Life Death Memories

Life Death Memories

Thomas T. Hecht

Leopolis Press
Charlottesville VA

Leopolis Press
530 Kellogg Drive
Charlottesville VA 22903-4642

Library of Congress Card Number: 2001098087
Hecht, Thomas T. 1929-
Life Death Memories

ISBN No:0-9679960-1-5
    p cm (paper: alkaline paper)
    1. Holocaust, Jewish (1939-1945), Poland
    2. Memoir, Holocaust survivor
    3.Poland, Busk, Ukraine, Jews, Ethnic relations

Table of Contents

Introduction

Irene Pipes

I have read and re-read Thomas T. Hecht's story. To me, what is most charming about it is that he wrote it looking back into and recreating a child's perspective. Writing with love, nostalgia and sadness, he evokes so many remembered details. It took years for the survivors of the Holocaust to write their memoirs. Although there are now many of these, each one tells us new facts and presents a different point of view. Their authors bring to us different experiences, joined together in being all horrible, and show us how all suffered, whatever the family background, profession, level of income, or area of what was then Poland long ago.

Such is this story.

It is set in the town of Busk; and my connection with Busk is very dear to me, since both my paternal grandparents, my father and all his brothers and sisters were born there. When I was four or five years old, my parents took me to visit my grandparents, who owned a large farm. My grandfather, a tall, bearded man, besides being a farmer was a very observant and learned Jew who was treated like a rabbi by his friends and neighbors. My grandmother, born Danziger, who wore a wig, was a small, quiet woman busy from morning to night with housework and feeding her large family. Our language in common was German, since they spoke Yiddish and German, and I spoke German and Polish. I remember going out on the farm and collecting a bouquet of many kinds of flowers and stalks of wheat, to take home with me. It went on top of an old, tall cabinet, awaiting the time for me to leave. To this day I remember how sorry I felt that I forgot to take it with us back to our home in Warsaw.

Some years ago, I interviewed one of my uncles about life in Busk; and all that Thomas Hecht describes about the village and its population of 10,000, one-third Jewish, very much agrees with what I heard from my uncle. He told me for example of the importance of Count Casimir Badeni, once the Prime Minister of Austria-Hungary, who built there a palace for himself and insisted that the railroad station be located six miles away in Krasne so that he would not be disturbed. He was friendly to the Jews and employed them on his estate.

On a trip to Poland in October 1986, I decided to visit Busk, for I was curious about my roots. This was still in the days of the Soviet Union, and travel in that region

Introduction

was not easy. I went by train from Krakow to Lwów. The authorities could not understand why I wanted to go to Busk and presented every possible difficulty, such as that there was no car available; but after two days of argument and my agreeing to pay an exorbitant amount, I was told that a small, rickety bus, and a driver, were ready for me. I found out later that Busk was off limits to foreigners. I did ask for a driver who spoke Polish but did not get one. I was lucky anyway to have a nice, energetic young man who spoke only Ukrainian; but since the two languages are quite similar, we understood one another. The main thing was that he understood why I was there and what I wanted to find. The Busk of today is not the shtetl of old.

Here are some excerpts from the diary I kept of the trip:

"The road to Busk is basically the road to Kiev and quite uninteresting. We passed a huge statue dedicated to 1939, the year Ukraine was 'liberated.' At the city entrance to Busk a large statue of a woman representing good harvest greeted us. The town itself had nothing but the very basic shops and one restaurant. The houses are all of brick and cement, built since the war; the old ones were either destroyed by the Germans or taken apart by the present government to make room for new housing. We drove around and around looking for someone old enough who would remember the days before the war. We were directed to a Mrs. Dawidowska...84 years old...yes, she remembered the

Life Death Memories

Danziger family; they were rich; they owned the local inn; one had a barber shop and another, a farm. She suggested we find a Mr. Zielinski, a local gossip. Yes, he said, the Danzigers were all over. He climbed into our bus and took us to Sukowa Street, where the farm had been. None of the old houses was left, but at least I now know where my father was brought up.

"He concluded with telling us that that the Germans rounded up 4,000 Jews from Busk and the surrounding area in the main square to be sent to death...."

Irene Pipes is President of the American Association for Polish-Jewish Studies. She is married to the distiguished Russian Historian, Richard Pipes, the Frank B. Baird Jr. Professor of History, Emeritus, at Harvard University.

The Shtetl

I may be on my way to my office, or to court, at some social event, or just at home, and my mind turns to that scene of my father and my brother during their last hours. My mind carries me back to Ulica Tarnowskiego, to the house where I was born and raised, at Tarnowskiego 9.

It is a street in Busk, formerly Poland, now Ukraine. I cannot help thinking of the street, and of when my dearest father and Lonek, my beloved brother Lonek, were passing our house on their way to the Jewish cemetery. Yes, the horse-drawn cart, and my father and Lonek inside. Was Lonek crying? And my father? Was he crying? Or were they already too frightened and exhausted to think of or to grasp the fact of death?

The cart-driver was a local man. He must have known my father. And the guards: what of their humanity? I ask myself: how, when and why did the cart-driver and the guards lose their humanity?

This event more than any other dwells indelibly in my mind and awareness. Almost to the last hours, and until it was too late, we did not believe what was happening. Yes, there were great hardships, very bad things were happening to us; and there were rumors of yet worse things happening in neighboring towns and villages. But we believed, I certainly believed, that we were special, that Busk was special, that we would come through alive.

But when not seeing the horse-drawn cart carrying my father and brother to their deaths, I can recall other images of life on my street and in my beloved little town.

The Shtetl

I had an uneventful childhood. My family loved me. We lived in a tightly knit community of Jews who knew our island place in the sea of anti-Semites. My father had a leather-goods store in the house where we lived. Thus, my parents were always home. My family was a large one. They and my paternal and maternal grandparents were born in Busk and lived in Busk all their lives.

Now I see my brother Lonek, and I see him, my beloved brother, in the act of hurling a pail of water from the front door of our house onto the street, water most likely from washing the floor. I can see his face, yes, the motion, the way he would hold the pail, the left hand outstretched holding the front of it, and his right hand under the bottom of the pail, heavy to the brim with water; and then he would hurl out its contents, just as I would have done.

My brother Lonek had a small scar near his upper lip from the time a horse had lightly kicked him. The same dear Lonek who, during a flood,

3

had fallen off the temporary bridge thrown up across our river Bug.

I did not love anyone so much as my brother Lonek. He was one year older than I. He was not my rival. He was too good to me. I knew that. To my surprise, he was always willing to share what he had with me. I couldn't understand it and cannot forget it. For instance, when he received Chanuka gelt, coins traditionally given to children during the Jewish Festival of Lights, I dared him to give me some of the groszen. He gladly gave me some. There was nothing I couldn't get out of him.

The most common expression one heard on the street, whether from other children or from grownups, was "kiss my ass." "Kish mach in tuchys" or "Pocaluj mie w dupe": it had a sing-song, sweet sound in the Polish language and especially so in Yiddish. I wondered why this saying or challenge seemed so common, and so daring. So I pulled down Lonek's pants and said, "Let me do it, let me kiss your behind." He let me, and

The Shtetl

I realized that there was nothing to it and that the expression was only a way to show that one was a grownup and free to say and do what one liked. Lonek and I couldn't stop laughing as we thought of the stupidity of grownups and of having done something forbidden. What stays with me is how my older brother was playful, and his willingness to listen to me and please me.

But then, at the shul, someone would set off a fight between us. We would wrestle and scratch each other. Usually, I think, I would prevail. I beat up my brother, and then I would feel strong but exhausted, and then badly about myself, especially when I saw his scratched-up, sweaty face.

Lonek had freckles. He was blond. Though he was one year older than I, we were about the same height and size. We could have passed for twins.

Those were good times to be growing up, before 1939, prior to the War. The center of my town Busk, the so-called rynek, consisted of buildings (mostly two or three story brick buildings with sheet-metal roofs) encircling a common area which was the market place. The market day was held on Thursday in this rather large space. There, merchants would put up stalls, and farmers from the surrounding villages would fill it with their horses, wagons, cows, chickens, fruits and vegetables, farm produce of all kinds. There farmers would sell as well as barter their commodities for fabrics, leather goods, sugar and the whole range of items available in the surrounding stores and stalls. Opposite stood a karczma or szynka, a bar, and to the side of the center of the market area there was a small structure surmounted with the figure of a stork, which was the emblem of my town Busk.

Flocks of storks often flew over the town. The children would sing: "Bocian leci, nie ma dzieci, a my mamy in nie odamy," (The stork is flying without its children, but we have them, and will keep them).

The Shtetl

There was another karczma close to the lumberyard owned by my uncles. When visiting my uncles at the lumberyard, I would always walk into the karczma, prepared with the excuse that it was just to say hello. What fascinated me was the tumult, the commotion made by the drunken, smoking, boisterous farmers. And without fail, one man, blind in one eye, would be sitting in a corner, dressed in the worn uniform of a Polish soldier, with his distinctive Polish soldier's cap. He would always be smiling while holding a big stein of beer. He would exclaim, seeing me, "Hey, Zydku, come here!" I would hesitate. And I would wonder, was he some hero, or just a Jew-hating Pole.

The owner (my mother's distant relative) would mumble complaints and curses at him in Yiddish, but she was powerless to throw him out.

But back to the karczma or szynk in the rynek. It was as a great secret that a friend excitedly told me that I would have a chance to taste a little mayd, the Yiddish word for a sweet thick type of brandy, something like slivovicz. I was curious; I was adventurous. So, I went into the karczma and met the son of the owner, who was in my view a grownup. I cannot remember whether he actually gave me or merely promised the drink. Anyway, he led me down the narrow, unlit staircase into a cold, dark cellar. There he took a wood panel, leaned it against a beer barrel, making a kind of seesaw, and pushed me against it. Breathing heavily, he hastily opened his trousers and rubbed against my thighs. It was damp; it was dark; it was lurid. I ran home. After that I never went there again.

I come back now, to more pertinent matters, to my beloved brother Lonek. Dumping dirty water out onto the street was a common practice. The water prevented clouds of dust from rising when horse-drawn carts rode by on the unpaved street. In fact, we sprinkled water over the dusty street and sidewalk to comply with an ordinance requiring us to sweep it. As luck would have it, however, Lonek's elementary school teacher was just approaching the front of our house when Lonek dumped out the pail of dirty water. The stream of water caught the teacher nearly full on. He made a terrible scene. Lonek cried and ran to hide. When he came out of his hiding place he was trembling with fright. The teacher, a notoriously frightening authority figure, scolded him severely. Lonek must have been traumatized by what happened. As if this were not enough, the teacher made my Lonek repeat the class year. Whether it was because of this incident or another unfortunate escapade, I became protective of him, as if I were the older brother.

The front entrance to our house led to my father's leather goods store, from which a door opened onto the living room. There also a side entrance to the living room. To the side of that room there was a small kitchen with the stove that every Jewish home had, specially constructed of hard limestone to keep warm the Sabbath and holiday meals, for cooking was not allowed on those days. On Fridays my mother would bake delicious potato "coggles" and other delicacies. Farther back, adjoining the living room, was a small bedroom. There was a small cellar in the kitchen, actually a hole in the ground, always damp, but sufficient to hold a few sacks of potatoes and other vegetables.

Around this time, before the War, the Polish authorities of the town began a campaign to keep the streets and other areas clean, so as to contain the spread of an epidemic of tuberculosis. In our store signs were posted saying, "Spluwaj do spluwaczki!", (spit into the spittoon!). I developed a certain fondness (was it because of the musical sound?) for the phrase "Spluwaj do spluwaczki." These particular words seemed meant for each other. And then the new rules about the necessity for cleanliness in front of one's house! A new pretext, I thought, for the anti-Semitic Polish policemen to harass the Jewish shopkeepers and homeowners. It was easy for a policeman to extract a bribe or, alternatively, to levy a fine. Besides the harsh new laws about cleanliness, we also experienced the rise of the Endek (National Democrats), a fascist Polish political organization. They put up signs saying "Jews to Palestine!" or "Don't buy in Jewish stores!" or "Jews to Madagascar!" and so on. One time, when I heard that a policeman was on his way up the hill of our street, writing out tickets for fines as he went, I grabbed the broom and ran into the street, putting all my strength into sweeping the dirt. Our road was a semi-dirt road that ran in front of our house. I applied the broom too hard, dislodging pebbles along with the dirt. Noticing this, my father ran out of the store and, with some impatience, grabbed the broom out of my hands, and showed me how foolish I was in the way I swept the street. I remember my embarrassment.

It was at this time, just before the War, that my father, and the small shopkeepers in the leather trade, were perplexed by a novel development in their line of business: ready-made foot-wear, something which was never heard of before. A Czech company, known as Bata, was opening stores selling ready-made shoes and boots, and therefore, according to my father, threatening our livelihood. And all this was happening in addition to the growing, virulent anti-Semitism.

My oldest brother Chuny was two or three years older than I. Though all three of us looked very much alike, I felt that Chuny kept his distance from me. How childish it was! Yet I must face up to it and admit that I did not like him. Oh, forgive me, brother, how I hated you! Of course, we now know about sibling rivalry. I always knew that I could handle my dear brother Lonek, that he was soft and had a good heart. On the other hand, the chasm between my brother Chuny and me was too great.

As intensely as I loved Lonek, I hated Chuny. I could not play with his friends. To me, he was a know-it-all. He knew everything. He was stronger. He ignored me and pushed me aside at his whim. I felt that I did not exist for him. I just hated him. And in the worst of times, even as we were cramped together in the Ghetto, hungry and scared for our lives, I still prayed to God to take him away from us. When the time came, when at the age of sixteen, he was taken away, after being brutally maimed, how did I feel about it? Were my evil thoughts in any way responsible for what happened to him?

Among the Jews in Busk, our street, Ulica Tarnowskiego, was known as the Shoychete-gass, the Ritual Slaughterer's Street. The Shoychete's house was two houses down from ours. The Shoychete plied his profession, which included the religious office of slaughtering fowl, in his small backyard. I had a good view of the women coming and going from his property. Under their arms, oftentimes hidden under their shawls, they carried the poor chickens on their way to having their throats slashed.

Life Death Memories

I was curious about what was going on and thus did not fail to observe the Shoychete in the expert practice of his craft. He would pull up and twist the chicken's head, pluck off some feathers from its neck, hold the beak between his fingers, say the ritual prayer, slash the helpless chicken's throat, then let the blood gush out into a pail. The poor dead chicken, drained of its blood, would be given back to its owner, who would then wrap it up in paper, pay the Shoychete some groszy, and with the dead chicken would be on her way.

Tarnowskiego Street was the main street leading from the small settlements on the south side of town to the marketplace, the rynek, as well as to the Polish church and the Ukrainian church. Thus, Christian funeral processions from the western and southern sides of town as well as from neighboring villages would pass by our house. There were many such Polish and Ukrainian Christian processions. The Christians paraded with colorful flags, icons, gongs, ornaments and images of Christ and Mary Immaculate. All this passed our house on Tarnowskiego Street.

The way to the Jewish cemetery also ran down our street, and it was the only way to get there. While a Christian funeral procession was a colorful, disciplined, and somber spectacle, a Jewish funeral was a gloomy, hurried affair. You would see a swiftly moving, closely-bunched group of people, clad in black, holding up a wooden platform or bier, with two protruding hand bars in front and two in the back, on which rested the box containing the deceased, wrapped in a white shroud. This belonged to the Jewish community and was stored in the basement of the synagogue. Following the scurrying men who carried the bier bearing the deceased were women wailing and throwing up their hands, lamenting the departed, or using the occasion to pray to God to send them help to alleviate their own miseries. The corpse lay wrapped in the white shroud, and the box was covered with a black cloth on which there were embroidered

Life Death Memories

Hebrew letters and a Magen David, or Star of David. There was also the shames, the sexton, rattling the coins in his collection box, asking the onlookers for a donation. At the same time he intoned a lament, still so familiar to me. I wish I could reproduce the melody or at least the words (it sounded like...hookaly-kookaly mavet... hookaly-kookaly mavet), and so it went on and on, and the rattle of the pushka, the collection box, with the coins inside making their own sound of woe. I never knew the meaning of the words, and in my memory of them, they may indeed have had no meaning at all. In it all there was the atmosphere of tragedy, chaos and, yes, harmony: the fast-paced bearers of the platform with the black-draped coffin, the women, members of the deceased's family, with their black shawls, tears flowing down their faces, raising their arms in lamentation, the crying women folk, the motley crowd trying to keep pace, the "hookaly-kookaly" of the shames with his rattling of the collection

16

box, the children and dogs running along; it all was so sad, yet there appeared in all that haste a determination swiftly to reach a destination, a place.

Our house was on the low part of a slope. In the wintertime it was great fun to slide down from the top of the street on a sled or primitive skis almost all the way to our house. My uncles were in the lumber business, and their carpenters made me a sled and skis. My dear father bought me skates on one of his trips to Lwów. The water that flooded the meadows would freeze over, as did the river Bug, and I would skate or ski a great part of the day during the long winter.

I remember the winter of 1938-1939. My father bought a building in Lwów to please my mother, whose ambition it was eventually to settle in the big city and to send her three sons to the Gymnasium in Lwów. And I had my dreams of being a help to my father, in fact, to expand his leather goods business so that even the great Polish Marshal Pilsudski would visit one of our stores and purchase his boots there. These were my visions and daydreams.

Spring arrived. Warming sun, melting snow, gushing waters, new clothes, new shoes for Passover. Yes, I have pleasant memories of growing up in Busk.

Only one row of houses separated my house from the languidly flowing river Bug. In the summer time we would frolic with the boys and girls on the banks of the river or try to catch fish and, of course, jump in or out of the river and swim. We even dared to jump into and out of the river naked to the greatest giggles and consternation of the girls.

Farther north from the riverbank there was a small lake. I could see beautiful white lilies floating on its calm waters. How I wanted to gather or at least touch these lilies! But somehow I was afraid to go so far out of my familiar surroundings.

My maternal grandfather, Oscar Goldberg, and my mother's five brothers, Abraham, Itzchak,

The Shtetl

Jacob, Tulu and Herman, and two step-siblings, Laiser and Henia, were all well off. My paternal grandparents and my father's two brothers and two sisters were also well off, that is, for the Jewish society in Busk. My mother's family were in the lumber business, and my father's family were storekeepers in leather goods. My grandfather's dwelling and leather goods shop were in the rynek. My other grandfather's lumberyard was on the outskirts of town. While growing up in Busk I knew that I could feel proud of the family I belonged to. I knew that they loved me.

My father was in his early twenties when he married my mother, who was then nineteen. They purchased from his father his father's old house at Tarnowskiego 9. I often heard it repeated that it was at the urging of my mother that my father became independent. My mother always bragged that it was to the credit of her initiative that the house was renovated and enlarged. My father worked with his father, my grandfather, until he left to establish his own leather-goods store. I overheard that originally my grandfather resented this. And for good reason, since the peasants on their way to the rynek would travel through our street and, seeing the store and the shingle emblazoned with my father's name, TOBIAS HECHT, go no farther for their leather merchandise.

In time, however, my grandfather loved to come to visit us and did so often. He was fun to have around, but he had his peculiarities. He was a simple man with simple habits. For instance, when he needed to urinate, he would go outside and do it against the fence, even though the outhouse was just steps away. When I complained, he would smile knowingly and say, "Never hold your pee." Trivial. But we had such times.

My paternal grandmother was very fond of me. To this day, I cannot forget her strong embraces, and also, of course, her special cybele kichlach, poppy seed and onion cookies, to which she always treated me. Besides the cybele kichlach and kisses, I cannot forget the picture of my grandmother lying in bed on Saturdays, when I religiously came to visit, and her reading in Hebrew from the pages of a huge book, a Midrash.

I loved to go to my grandparents' house, where two of my father's brothers also lived with my grandparents. Yichiel was a year or two younger than my father, and Moiszaly was younger by several years. Yichiel was married and lived with his wife and two little boys on the upper floor.

The memory of Yichiel's boys is with me; the oldest, I recall now, was Rysio, yet shamefully, I have forgotten my other cousin's name. I think that I would recognize both of them. Or would I? Often I look at lively, boisterous, blond children in a playground and search for the faces of my now non-existent cousins. Of course I know that the playing children are not my cousins. It only reminds me how my mother would look for years on the street at faces with the hope of encountering the face of her husband and sons, though she knew that her search was in vain. The Germans killed Rysio, his little brother, his father and mother during the first Aktion. I do not have my cousins' pictures, just as no pictures have survived of my father or my grandparents. Their likeness persists only in some part of my memory.

Yichiel's wife Fanka came from the big city of Lwów. She was what we would call a snob, feeling herself superior to those around her. I can just imagine that my strong-willed grandmother did not give her an easy time, living in the same house as they did. But then my grandmother was not that fond of my mother either, resenting my mother's influence over my father and, especially, his leaving the family business. She would have preferred that my father had remained under her thumb, like Yichiel and Moiszaly.

My grandfather, as I did not fail to notice, was very fond of my mother. When he came to visit, they would tease each other, joke and laugh.

The Shtetl

Fanka, my stuck-up aunt, belittled me when, at seven or eight, I still could not tell time. On a dresser in her messy upstairs apartment, there stood a black figurine with a clock embedded in it. I gasped in fright at my first sight of this unnatural spectacle and thereafter tried not to look at it. But this was hard, because it stood in the only room where I could play with my two little cousins.

In our home we had no paintings or pictures, let alone figurines or sculptures. Nor was there anything like that anywhere I went, except of course for the terrifying nailed-to-the-cross Christ on the front wall of the classroom of the Polish school I attended. Just before the War, in 1938, I went to Lwów on a school trip to see a famous Panorama that depicted famous historic and heroic battles of the Polish people and its army. The painting was on a huge canvas hung on a circular wall. One walked on a platform around the canvas. The Panorama had soldiers in battle, blood spilling, drawn sabers, rifles with bayonets, cannons, galloping horses with their riders, men and horses jumping, turning, falling, and dying, battle flags, and fields and villages in flames. All this made a deep impression on me. I walked out of the Panorama, not accustomed to city streets, and right into a telephone pole. I came home with a big blue bump on my forehead, but bigger still in my mind were the sights of Lwów and the disturbing scenes of the Panorama.

Other than reading the prayers, I do not believe that my grandfather could read or write. Oh, yes, he could count, I am sure; and he knew his business. My father's competition did not hurt grandfather's business. Both did well.

Grandfather and father both enjoyed high esteem in the community. They had what was called yches, an honorific appellation earned by one's charitable deeds, character and comportment. They owned permanent seats in the Temple, which they had bought outright. The ownership of the seats and their location testified to their social standing. My grandfather belonged to the "Old Temple." My father belonged to the main and newer Temple. Each had a seat directly facing the bima, or podium, closest to the side where the Torah scrolls were kept. It was in the same row as the Rabbi's seat and was in fact close by. The bima was in the middle of the Temple floor; the Torah scrolls were kept by the eastern wall.

My great joy was to walk to the Temple with my father. We held hands, talking or chanting melodies. On those walks, I felt that my father belonged to me and to me only, and that the world belonged to me. In the Temple I loved to rub my finger on the bronze plate affixed to the book-stand and engraved in Hebrew letters with my father's name.

As my memories bring me to the Temple, I stress that all Jews in Busk and, indeed, all the Jews in the shtetlach were God-fearing, observant Jews. There was no such thing as branches of Judaism. Some were more strictly observant, some less so.

Some were followers of a particular Rabbi and were known as chusyds. Some of the less observant may even have dared to eat ham or kielbasa or smoke during the Sabbath. Yes, there were apycoires, or sinners, but we were all one community.

Jewish boys, with few exceptions, were sent to a chaider, a religious school, at age three and up. This custom was changing, just before the War, when Zionist organizations started Hebrew schools. The chaider was conducted at the shul or at the house of the melamed, the teacher. My career at the chaider was very short. I hated the melamed. He was a big, bearded, uncouth brute. Once he made some disparaging remark about me or my family. Deep down, I knew that I could find a way to stop attending the chaider. So I told my parents about the offensive remark of the melamed's. I succeeded in changing to the newly formed Hebrew school instead. The studious, pale little kids who wore payes, side-curls, and an

undergarment with laptzydeklach, fringes, continued as always in the chaider.

At home we spoke Yiddish, but not exclusive-
ly, for we also spoke Polish. The more observant
Jews were less exposed to the non-Jewish population. This was a great disadvantage during the
Holocaust. The more Orthodox girls, by custom, were even more tied to their immediate
families and rituals and thus were less likely to
be able to hide their identities on Aryan papers,
since they spoke Polish or Ukrainian with a
detectable accent. The men clung to their own
rituals and, besides, had difficulties with language, attire and kashrut; in short, the more
observant were less likely to have made contacts
with the Aryan population. They were the first
to fall victim to the exterminations.

In its time, the Temple was a place for joy and
for spiritual awe. Joyfully we met boys and girls
our own age, everyone dressed in their best
clothes. We met uncles and numerous cousins.

Grandparents and uncles and aunts hugged us. And there we came to be with God, and to send thoughts and wishes in chants and prayers consisting above all of praise for the Almighty, as if He needed our praises in order to fulfill our wishes.

There were joyous holidays like Purim, Pesach, and Symchas Torah. But then! Oh, the crying, the wailing on Yom Kippur! The fear and anxiety of Judgment Day flooded every cell of the body. Before the Day of Awe, it was a tradition to submit oneself to flagellation at the Temple. How scary it was to see my father stretched out on top of a layer of straw on the floor of the Temple, scourged with long branches by the shames, the shul attendant. I believe it was meant to be penance for his sins. Then there was the ritual of Keppuris, or Kapparah. My father called each of his children inside. I came close to him, and he held me close. In his hand he held a chicken. My father then raised the arm with the chicken in his hand and whirled the chicken over my head, at the same time saying a prayer. The chicken was meant as an offering to God, a spiritual cleansing and an expiation for sins.

On the Day of Atonement all Jews would congregate in the Temple and pray all day. The air inside was filled with smoke from hundreds of burning candles. The rabbi came dressed all in white, without shoes, wearing white socks. The men wore their prayer shawls over their heads. Everyone swayed while praying. The women in their section, in the gallery, cried loudly. How could God in heaven not hear these supplicants! Everyone fasted. One had a vision of God sitting on high with His pen, registering in the open book who should live and who should die. So it was from year to year, and filled with awe.

The summer of 1939 came to an end. Up the hill of my street Mr. Raubfogel had a radio. Neighbors would gather to listen to the screeching sounds coming from that strange box. There was talk of the Danzig Corridor, of War, of

Life Death Memories

Mobilization. That last word was frightening
and came out in hushed sounds. Then the word
Mobilization became a reality. Stillness descend-
ed on the town. Refugees from the western parts
of Poland hurried through town bent on escaping to the East. Some, seeking shelter, stayed in
Busk. It did not take a struggle. Then the Red
Army arrived.

The main street in Busk ran through the
rynek, the town center. It was part of the highway
leading from Lwów all the way east to Brody, and
on to Kiev. Once, while I was walking with my
brother Lonek, at the curve just outside the
rynek, our Zabka, our white-and-brown spotted
dog, was ripped open by a passing Red Army
truck. The bloody innards burst out, while our
dear, dying pet Zabka wailed. I wished, even then,
that Lonek could have been spared this terrible
sight. Always so sensitive, he was heartbroken
and grieved for a long time.

The Shtetl

On this main road through the rynek there was a steeper hill atop which, facing west, was the palace of the Hrabia, or Count, Badeni. Busk was in fact famous in Galicia because of Hrabia Badeni piwo, Badeni beer. The Count owned extensive properties in and around Busk, including his famous brewery. His castle was surrounded by a tall iron fence, which started at the bottom of the hill by the old mill, and continued all the way to the top. The fence ended at a huge, decoratively carved iron gate. There were trees and meadows behind the fence. The palace itself was set back on wide grounds behind gardens and big, old trees. Toward the back of the palace grounds, yet close to the fields and stream, was the brewery.

During the time of these events, the Hrabia Badeni was absent. First the Russian soldiers, then, later, the German army and the SS occupied the palace. During the German occupation, I was among those recruited to pluck hops for the brewery.

Reader, please be patient with me now. As I go on, I want to mention a few names and scenes. Probably the only trace of the earthly existence of those who had these names is the memory of them which I carry. In most cases, I carry in my memory only pictures of the children and the teenagers like me; many of the names, alas, have faded with the years. The children, the teenagers, the adults once existed: then their lives were snuffed out.

Some of these memories are digressions. They are glimpses from ordinary times in my life growing up as a Jewish boy in the days before 1939, in a small town in Eastern Europe, in what was then Poland, and is now Ukraine. Were it not for the events that followed, my growing up, even my entire life, would be rather ordinary. But what was special, and tragically so, is what happened to those to whom this writing is dedicated, to those human beings, both simple ones and exceptional ones, whose lives were taken away. Some could have contributed much to the world; all of them deserved to live.

And my own feelings of unworthiness in comparison to some who perished were clear to me even as a young boy. What I have set myself to do is to write a Memorial for those I loved, for those I knew. And for many, many more still, whom I did not know personally, and for whom there is no survivor who could speak for them and say that, at a time not so long ago, they did truly live upon this earth.

We were given a life to live, which in itself is an all-encompassing mystery. And there we were, ordinary people with no ideology. We had our religion, our beliefs and our customs. None of us was threatening others. As I said, we were ordinary people, leading ordinary lives; loving, struggling, suffering. Not one of us asked to be born, yet once alive, we struggled mightily to hold on to life. What compels me in this telling is how, during these times, we were not allowed to live our lives. Why? The sole reason for this was that in a certain place and at a certain time, we were born Jews, and there were those armed with both hatred and guns who took upon themselves the obligation to kill the Jews.

And so, under the German occupation, the time came for the formation of the Ghetto. This was in an area of the town picked by the German authorities without regard for the space actually needed, into which all of the town's Jews, and also the Jews from the neighboring villages, were crammed to make the segregated area called the Ghetto. There came the time of hunger and typhus, the time when we, emaciated, impotent, frightened, the Ghetto dwellers, became like condemned animals, facing the sentence of death passed by law against all Jews. Yes, the sentence, decreed by the German authorities, and carried out with all the efficiency available to a modern 20th Century state.

The Shtetl

What constantly fills my mind needs finally to come out and be shared with others. I owe this telling to all those of my small town, Busk, and also to all those who were murdered and of whom neither name nor trace is left. Only the living can speak. I feel compelled to set forth what follows:

When I mention only a name or refer to someone whose name I have forgotten, please remember I am referring to a life: a child, a mother or father, a future not fulfilled, a part of society, a person with feelings whose life was cut short. I tell here of some of my experiences. During those tragic times, experiences like mine were shared by those who were cruelly murdered. The final picture, the final tears and cries, this they alone took with them to their common pit of death. Can I, or anyone else, tell how my friends felt standing before their graves? Of course not! But I must say, in their honor, in their memory, for nothing else is left of them, that they, the Jewish children, brothers, sisters, fathers, mothers and their extended families existed on this earth, and that their lives were summarily taken from them, and only because they were born Jews.

What follows is neither artfully wrought nor other than what I perceived. It is a pouring out of memories. It is my meager tribute to the dead. I am setting this down also with the thought that someone might encounter this narrative, contemplate it, and learn from it. Will my beloved grandchildren read this? They are so much on my mind. How much do I want them, and you, reader, to contemplate the miracle of Life, the most precious gift there is in the world! Life!

There existed a Hanusia, a Shayele, a Yoynele, and so many laughing and happy children: and mothers, fathers, uncles and aunts, cousins and friends. Their lives were snatched from them. I, the lucky one, have been strutting through my days, but with my memory full of them, and my heart filled with love for them.

The Shtetl

There were my paternal grandparents, Heschel and Peria, who were born and lived all their lives in Busk, and were killed in the nearby woods. There were my father's two married sisters, one named Chaya, I don't recall my other aunt's name; there was one married brother, Yichiel, each of whom had several children. There was my father's single brother, Moishele, who was eighteen when he was killed. My mother lost three brothers, Itzchak, and Laiser, both single, and Herman, his wife Mina, and their beautiful child Hanusia. There are no memorials for any of them. Of my former friends, no one survived. Of those my own age, only two are left.

I wish I could find a painter who could fix this one scene, so strongly locked in my memory: the horse-drawn carriage, the guards, the local farmer. There, in the middle, my beloved father and my brother Lonek passing our house on Ulica Tarnowskiego on their way to the Jewish cemetery. What were their thoughts and feelings?

Life Death Memories

Were they permitted to embrace? Were they crying? Did they still cling to some hope?

39

The Russians

During the Russian times, before the German occupation, in the winters of 1939-1941, and usually on that main road, I would be skating. Sometimes I hitched onto a passing army truck which was lumbering slowly up the hill. The truck would pull me to the top. Then from the top by the palace, I would let go and skate back downhill, repeating the fun for hours. My friends Shulu and Hesiu were with me. They were very adept at this sport. Often a soldier on a truck would kick off the homemade wire hook or the gloved hand that grasped the rear of the truck, but then I would just hook on to another. It was fun, though now I realize it was a dangerous sport; for a truck could skid on the ice or snow, and before realizing it one could be crushed behind the wheel or run over by another truck, which was usually part of an army convoy.

My fun-loving friends and I were daredevils. I learned many tricks from Shiulu. There were five of us, who were inseparable. In fact, later, when the Germans arrived, we named ourselves the "Red Five." Needless to say, our gang did not last long. A few of my friends, among them Hesiu, were murdered by the Germans in the first Aktion, the name for a roundup of Jews for extermination.

To everyone in Busk I was called by my nickname Ciupka. My Hebrew name was Israel. To my grandparents, I was Srulikel, a Yiddish diminutive for Israel, though my name, with time, went through other changes.

We were under Russian rule from September 1939 to July 1941. In the West, a war was raging.

The Russians

There was also a war between Russia and Finland. I avidly followed the news about this war and rooted for the Russians. I loved the Russian songs. I loved the Russian idea that all people were equal; that is, Jews were the same as all and should not be mistreated. That was the theory. I loved to watch the marching and singing Russian soldiers. I was fascinated when the soldiers paraded through the town; the lieutenant, marching alongside, shouted his commands, and the soldiers responded in unison.

But, it is true, personal frustrations and conflicts arose. My family was of the bourgeois class. I had to reconcile my love for my father with the propaganda at school which taught that we must hate the bourgeois, who were the enemies of the proletariat. In school we were told of a new world coming, when the proletariat would have inevitably prevailed in the class struggle. We were taught to glorify only the working class and to join the battle against the merchants, the capitalists: the very class I came from.

This indoctrination taught us to love only batyko, father Stalin. Stalin, indeed, we were told, was our true father. The enemies of the proletariat and their exploiters, so we were to believe, were, like my father, people of the bourgeois class. And we were to be always on guard and vigilant when in contact with these enemies of the people. We were to report any counterrevolutionary activities to the authorities. Such was the incessant indoctrination. Counterrevolutionary activities included any insults to the Communist Party, the regime, the proletariat or its exalted leaders.

I became a Young Pioneer, the first step on the path to membership in the Communist Party. I was found worthy by my Russian teacher, and in a moving ceremony I was awarded the distinctive red scarf worn only by the Pioneers. Silently, however, I prayed that my father might be spared and not be sent to Siberia. Many like him were picked up during the night and deported.

I was being indoctrinated to hate my father and my family because they were storekeepers and "capitalists." I was to be ashamed of my background, because my family were exploiters of the working classes, the cause of all the evil in the world. If I became so privileged, I was to join the Communist Revolution, which would prevail once the bourgeois class was eliminated.

Many local young men fell for this propaganda and its promise of utopia. But they lost their lives when they joined or were drafted into the Red Army. They were given no training, nor were they properly armed, and in that condition eventually went to fight the Germans. Their cause was just, but they were exploited and used as cannon fodder.

During the Russian occupation the Red Army garrison set up a field hospital in the yard of the Ukrainian church. One day I came upon a curious scene. There was no school for me then, and my friends and I went all over town. Through an opening in the fence, I watched a cadaver stretched out on a green military cot. A military doctor and a group of his assistants were standing around it. They were just in front of me when one of the doctors cut and pulled the skin from the cadaver's head. I stood there shocked and sickened, then pulled myself away.

Another time, a couple of Oriental-looking Russian soldiers, perhaps Mongols or Tartars, as were many of the Red Army soldiers I saw, waved to me on the riverbank, and took me into their rubber dinghy. They launched the dinghy in the rather slow-flowing water of our river Bug and paddled upstream. Then, after a distance, we turned around and floated back down.

As we approached a bend in the river, I became scared to death, because beyond it lay a dam and the huge turbines of Busk's electric power plant. The dam was behind the bend and completely invisible to the soldiers, who by now were drunk and feeling very jolly. We were floating ever faster, and they were carrying on and singing ever louder, while I was terrified of falling over the dam and being ground up in the turbines. How was I to tell them of the danger? I did not speak their language and did not want to appear to be a sissy. But as the rowing became more difficult and the rowboat's speed slowed, the soldiers realized that something was amiss. They pulled over to the bank and released me; and I showed them what was behind the river bend. They laughed, pulled up the dinghy from the water, and gave me a strong bear hug.

The low-lying meadows were flooded during the long and wet fall, and then froze over in the winter, along with the river Bug. We skated. We had fun in Busk in those days. When the thaw came, rivulets would stream down from the top of our street, carving out tunnels underneath the mounds of snow. Spring again brought floods from melting snow and ice.

One day, after sunset, I failed to return home, and my father came out with a search party. They found me and a friend or two a great distance away and in great distress. The ice had broken up during the afternoon, and I had floated away on an island of ice. All around us the ice was thin, the water deep, and the ground underneath soggy and treacherous, like quicksand. I had no way to get to higher ground until help arrived.

The Russian Communist propaganda did not alter my strong belief in our God. The belief remained, though in a deeper stratum of consciousness. But events to come changed all that.

My father was not in any way in local politics. But as for giving to charity or lending money to a neighbor or friend in trouble, my father could always be counted on. Even later, while in the Ghetto, an impoverished shoemaker, a Pole, to whom my father used to send work before the War, came to him to "borrow" money. He needed it for his wife's funeral. My father gave him the money. Regrettably, however, when at a later time we were desperately in need of his help he was either too scared or not clever enough to help us.

There was endemic anti-Semitism in the pre-War days. I have mentioned earlier that Polish anti-Semites, especially a group called the Endeks, would hand out fliers saying, "Don't buy from Jews!", "Jews to Palestine!", "Jews to Madagascar!" or "Away with the Jews!"! The word Zyd, Jew in the Polish language, is pejorative, venomous, implying: dirty, inferior, less than garbage. In the school the Polish and Ukrainian pupils would invariably gang up together, harass and beat up the Jewish pupils; and equally the teachers would single out a Jewish child to make fun of his or her accent or attire or find any pretext to hit the Jewish child with the cane the teacher would customarily be holding. On my way to school I would try to reach it through side streets or little-used paths so as to be all alone and in silence make my supplications to God to be spared the teacher's cane or other molestations. Windows of Jewish homes or stores were constantly broken. On national or religious holidays, there would always be anti-Jewish events and harassment.

As a child, very often, my heart felt very heavy. This gloom, this heaviness of heart of a child! I would soak up the worries of my parents and the events surrounding me. When factory-made shoes first arrived in stores, especially the Bata brand, I worried for my father's business. When a robbery occurred, or a Jew was beaten up, or a Jewish window was broken, or a Jewish house was set on fire or someone in the family became ill, it placed an additional stone in my heart. Then the Russians came and the source of my anxieties changed. I was no longer to be proud of my family, because it belonged to a caste considered an enemy of the people.

I was ten years old when Poland was partitioned, and the Red Army occupied Busk and its surroundings. The Polish school became a Ukrainian school. Our mode of existence changed drastically. We had to shun the Temple and stop religious practice. My father became a laborer, no longer to be considered a well-respected member of the community. We lived in fear of being placed on a transport to Siberia. Two of my uncles were arrested on trumped-up charges. How can I describe it? I loved and feared the new regime at the same time.

Then a great novelty came to Busk. A small biplane landed in a nearby field, ready to take on sightseers and fly above the surrounding countryside. My uncle Jacob sought me out, and we ran to the field where the plane had landed. We rode in a plane for the first time in our lives; it was indeed a great event in those days. In today's terms it was like flying to the moon. My grandmother, in fact, was astounded that anything but a bird could fly, and she did not believe me when I told her that a plane could fly even above the clouds. She thought it was impossible, for she believed that only God resided above the clouds.

During the summer the Russians brought several truckloads of the most delicious melons to Busk. We had never heard of or seen melons before. Rumors were that they came from Georgia or some other southern lands of Great Russia.

In the school the Russians introduced singing and dancing, as well as competitions in them. This was all new, and contrasted with the Polish school, which I hated. So I was on my way to becoming a great patriot. But could I be forgiven or overcome my bourgeois background? Could I be accepted even though I was not of the proletariat class? My father had owned a store. Thus we were exploiters, capitalists, and enemies of the state. It took me a long, long time to erase from my psyche negative feelings about commerce, money, capitalism and any activity other than physical labor.

The Russians

Once a Russian officer came to visit us. He was a physician and a Jew. During their conversation I overheard him say to my parents that all Russia is "one big cemetery." Often I mulled over this statement without understanding what the officer meant. Many years later, I came to understand it, and then only after my mind had opened to new ideas free of Russian propaganda.

Around the time the Red Army entered Busk, in September 1939, a middle-aged couple, who were distant relatives from western Poland fleeing from the Germans, came to live with us. But they were deported to Russia and died in Siberia. Many refugees came from the west. Some settled in Busk; some kept traveling east. For some reason the Russians branded these refugees as enemies and arranged transports which took them to Siberia. As fate would have it, a great percentage of this group did survive the War. Had they not been shipped off to Russia, most would have perished at the hands of the Germans and their allies.

53

Life Death Memories

We did not get along easily with some of the children of the refugee families who came to Busk from the western territories which had been invaded by the German armies. In a way, they were more sophisticated. They came mostly from cities, and we were very provincial. They seemed to have an accent, and it was a shock that some did not even speak Yiddish.

We teased the boys of these families. They couldn't do a local tongue-twister as fast as we could without a slip: "Fyn Alesk bys ka Bysk trukt a foks a byks in pysk" (From Alesk to Busk the fox carries the rifle in its mouth). The ability to perform this tongue-twister typed you as a true Galicianer, someone from our area of southeastern Poland. This area was dotted with small Jewish towns and villages. In my mind I see the happy young boys and girls who smiled and chattered, and played; loved Busk and loved being alive, yet whose lives were soon to be snuffed out. Nothing remains of most of them. Not a marker in a cemetery. Remember, in a past not distant from us, a German government decreed that these children, their parents and all Jews should not exist. Then they proceeded to carry out that decree.

While we were still under the Russian administration, a Russian engineer requisitioned one of the rooms of our house and moved in with a local woman of a certain sort. He was part of a team exploring for oil in and around our fields and meadows. He was a quiet man, but because he was an authority figure, an occupier, he was a bad fit with our tightly knit family. His face was always flushed, his working clothes smelly and dirty. I was dying of curiosity to see what he did in that back room. Often I tried to spy on them, as I expected to see something lurid. He and his woman spent most of the time in their room. I didn't see much. I imagined it had to do with drinking and with what men and women do. I was very curious, knowing lots of words about sex, but ignorant of details.

55

Life Death Memories

My mother had the courageous idea to hide some of the leather goods from our store inventory. She did this when the Red Army was about to occupy Busk. It helped us greatly later on when we would trade the leather for food and soap.

Once a train bound for Romania with treasures belonging to the collapsing Polish government was held up and its contents stolen. A peasant brought us a pile of silver utensils engraved with the Polish eagle. Among them were huge serving forks, dinner forks, smaller forks and spoons, large, small and tiny dessert spoons, and an entire range of utensils and other silver. My mother made a deal with the peasant and traded the silverware for packages of our hidden leather goods. Later on, some of this remaining cache was hidden in the back room behind a false fireplace.

The Germans

I think now of late summer, 1941, when Germany suddenly started its Blitzkrieg against Russia. While I was sitting on a bench with my oldest brother in the marketplace, a German plane dropped a bomb nearby. Apart from the awful, frightening sound of the explosion, there was no damage. I cannot forget my brother's exclamation as, scared, we ran for cover: "We are witnessing history in the making!" Witnessing history. This exclamation stuck with me. For years I pondered how my brother came to express such an intelligent and prophetic thought.

Life Death Memories

During the first days of the War, able-bodied people, among them my father, were taken away to dig ditches as defenses against German tanks. But they soon came back home.

Some, mostly young and single, who sympathized with the Soviets and who seriously believed the stories circulating about German atrocities against Jews, went eastward with the Red Army. One of my uncles hired two or three wagons with their peasant owner-drivers. We loaded up our most essential belongings in an attempt to go east to escape the Germans. But soon enough the futility of running away became obvious, for they were advancing faster than we could escape them. So we returned home.

The Red Army hurriedly retreated. Day and night, long columns of Russian soldiers filled the roads leading east. Soldiers marched on foot or rode on trucks, bicycles or horses. Tanks roared past. They pulled field kitchens and all types of military gear. Civilians trying to escape with the

The Germans

Red Army joined the flood of escapees, all fleeing the oncoming German hordes.

We were huddled at home anticipating unknown impending disaster. I heard the unmistakable deep thunder of an explosion. Then there was an eerie silence. Later I learned what had caused it. A small Russian tank had been positioned at the bottom of the hill to the side of the old mill near a sharp curve on the road. A German tank had hit the poor little tank from the top of the hill, causing the magazine to explode and the tank to burst into flames. Often I passed the carcass of the little tank and wondered what had happened to its crew. I wondered if they had been careless to park at the foot of the hill, where they were an easy target.

At the end of summer, the Germans arrived.

The following night there was pounding on our outer doors and shutters. There were vile curses and screams in Ukrainian: "Open the door, Zyd! Zyd!" It is hard to explain the venom the word "Zyd" carried with it. It meant "Less than human"; it meant "You vermin"; it meant, "I can step on you and kill you; you are dirt; you killed Christ, my God; and I must kill you." I tumbled out of my sleep and ran toward the door. In the dark I made out my father already standing there. I felt his body shaking in fear. The darkness of the night blanketed his face, but I felt his pallor and anxiety. Here was my strong, beloved father, my protector, shaking from fright, falling apart, at a loss. I clung to him as if my body would lend him some strength and lessen his paralysis. To open the bolted outer door, or not to open the door? He undid the latches of the outer door. The militiaman flung the door back. He was a Ukrainian, a local person, in work clothes because his militia hadn't yet received its uniforms. He came in and berated my father, claiming that gunshots had been heard coming from our house. This was a total lie. On this pretext he took my father to the police station. He was released the following day, after paying a ransom.

We were afraid of pogroms; we were afraid of looting. But there were no pogroms. We were spared. My conviction grew that nothing bad could ever happen in my town of Busk.

We learned that prior to abandoning the town, the Russian NKVD had arrested several Ukrainian nationalists. An army truck with a loudspeaker blasting out music had been parked outside the prison. Those inside were executed while the music drowned out the sounds of gunfire. We Jews had cause to fear retaliation, a pogrom, because the Jews were blamed for everything; and this crime had happened right in our Busk.

The Ukrainians set up a town administration. The Germans settled into the palace of Hrabia Badeni and a nearby building. For the time being, there was calm.

One of my uncles, Itzchak, an intellectual, was known among us as "the philosopher." He had

Life Death Memories

attended the Gymnasium in Kamionka Strumilowa, the county seat. In Busk there was only one public school, which went up to seventh grade. There were also one or more chaiders. Then, just before the War, from about 1936, a Hebrew school was founded, which I attended after regular school hours. It met only two or three afternoons a week and taught only the Hebrew language, unlike the chaider, where instruction was in the Hebrew prayers and scriptures.

Before the War, Uncle Itzchak had published privately a pamphlet entitled *Justification of a Religious Outlook on Life*. Inside its green covers there were a variety of mathematical formulas, mysterious to me, references to the speed of light, etc., and long words and sentences. The whole family took pride in the acknowledgment Professor Albert Einstein had sent to Itzchak of his having received a copy of it. I don't think any-one in the family was capable of understanding the contents of this pamphlet, nor the significance or eminence of Professor Einstein. Nevertheless, I was in awe of this achievement and assured myself that I would try to understand it when I grew up. The pamphlet survives to this day. Regrettably though, after what happened, not much survived of Itzchak's search for a "Justification of a Religious Outlook on Life."

Now, uncle Itzchak wrote a long letter in German, a missive of welcome. He gave it to me and asked me to go to the main street of our town and deliver it to any approaching German officer. Obediently, although with hesitation, I took the letter to the marketplace and, in time, approached a strolling German officer. He was a tall, lean man dressed in an imposing uniform and decorated cap. He wore shiny boots. To me he appeared to be a superman. I handed him the letter and ran away in fright. I mention this incident to show how naive my uncle Itzchak was. A multitude were like him. Some time later, uncle Itzchak just gave himself up to the Germans. He did not bother to try to escape or even to enter the hiding place we had in our house, when the Aktion finally came.

During this interim period, prior to the formation of the Ghetto, I roamed the streets and alleys of Busk, alone or with my best friends. My little cousin Shayele, five years old, was always attached to me like a loving puppy. He just loved to be with me, and I loved him. Shayele's father, who was my uncle Abraham, had been taken away by the Russians in one of their transports. I taught poor little Shayele to keep his mouth shut on seeing a stranger approach us, especially when we were walking on the edge of town. He always obediently did so, and always with a conspiratorial smile. He would then look up at me with his big, black, sad needy eyes, indicating that he understood the situation. I was afraid that a Gentile might detect an identifying Jewish accent if we were overheard talking to each other. Why expose ourselves to danger?

The Germans

We Jewish children also had a superstition that, if a priest or nun passed by while our mouths were open, our teeth would fall out. And of course there were many priests and nuns. My little Shayele and his delicate, loving mother Rachel were taken away to the death camp at Belzec and never heard from again.

As I mention Rachel, I can see her, as so often I do in my recollections, walking down the hill on our street, carrying a package before her with both arms. I wondered what she was carrying. She was clearly hurrying down the deserted street towards our house. I ran after her to see. She entered our home. My dear Rachel had brought us a cake. It was Purim. This she did in the midst of starvation, and persecution and death all around us.

While German military convoys moved eastward, another stream of bedraggled and emaciated men trudged homeward, having left Russian prisons or deserted from the Red Army. My uncle Herman was among them. He came home after having been imprisoned on some charges the Russian occupation had fabricated. During that time it did not take much to be sent to prison or Siberia.

In 1938, uncle Herman had built a beautiful house on the outskirts of town. The house was located on a road leading to Krasne, where the railroad station was. His house was the most modern house in Busk. Adjacent to it there was a large plot of land. When uncle Herman was still in prison, his wife Mina, who lived there with her beautiful three-year-old daughter, often asked me to, or asked my parents to let me, sleep over, which I did. The spaciousness of the house, the modernity of the rooms, the novelty of all that was there made up for my fear and resentment at having to be so far away from my beloved home. On one frightening occasion, however, a sudden draft caused a door to slam, catching two of my fingers between the door and its frame and cutting through my flesh to the bone. The flow of blood was frightening. To this day I have a scar on those fingers.

Shortly after uncle Herman returned from prison he came over to our house and asked me to help him clean up the adjoining lot and dig it up for what was to be a garden. I felt proud that he called on me to do a manly job. The pride did not last long. I was clearing the land and spading it up with all my energy until I could not go on. I suddenly felt a piercing pain in my testicles. I was ashamed to tell Herman that I had to stop. Herman was a man of few words. He seemed at least to me unapproachable. I dropped the shovel and left in shame and pain. When I came home I was put to bed. My testicles were swollen, perhaps from an infection. I never had a chance to tell Herman that it was not laziness that had caused me to disappoint him by not staying with the job, and that I was not a shirker.

Life Death Memories

All this happened before the formation of the Ghetto. It was a time when I would still run around with friends and seek excitement. I was secretly in love with Pepcia Fink. I fantasized that Pepcia would become my wife. Her father was a dealer in gypsum rocks. He would sell these huge white rocks mostly to peasants. When mixed with water, the gypsum turned to a white paint. My friends and Pepcia's friends teased us about being "boyfriend and girlfriend" and "being in love with each other," whatever that meant. Pepcia had red cheeks, big eyes, black hair, two long thick braids, lovely thick lips, and budding little breasts. I believed she knew my secret and that I dreamed about her. I believed that I was her favorite.

Pepcia's home and her family's business were in the rynek, the marketplace. On Thursday market day in Busk, Mr. Fink's place was mobbed. He weighed out chunks of gypsum, and the peasants loaded the rocks onto their horse-drawn carts. White dust flowed all over. I was fascinated by

The Germans

Mr. Fink. He had lost one eye when a wet, searing speck of gypsum had fallen into it, and the eye had just melted away.

During this period of lull before the Ghetto, on the same street on which I handed over the welcoming letter to the German officer, one day when I was with a group of friends, Pepcia came skipping by with a group of her friends. There we were, a meeting of two confused, bashful, opposing parties. To this day I cannot understand what impelled me. Nor can I forgive myself. Suddenly I teased Pepcia and cut off one of her beautiful long braids.

She was shocked. She cried. She ran after me as if to beat me for my outrage. I ran away with shame. My shame for my dastardly deed increased as time went on. I had no chance to beg her for forgiveness. The last time I saw Pepcia, she was running in panic with her grandmother, running through the backyard of my house. A rumor had reached her family that an Aktion was

71

about to begin. Seeking shelter, she and her grandmother ran away from the center of Busk to the outskirts. To this day, I remember my feeling of surprise, no, sorrow, powerlessness and deep sadness. Pepcia, running, scared, did not look at me. I felt so diminished. It occurred to me at the same time that she too must have felt embarrassed to be seen running in fright with her old grandmother. It was no longer a matter of boyfriend, girlfriend, or my silly prank, for which I cannot forgive myself; but for both of us now it became a matter of running away, of having to hide, of running to save one's life.

Another incident that caused me regret and for which I did not have the opportunity to apologize is the trick I played on my friend Iziu. Iziu was a boy my age, but smaller, a timid boy who liked to hang around me. He was a stepbrother of my beloved aunt Rachel. I egged him on to come with me without telling him where. Iziu should have known better; he should not have trusted me.

The Germans

Perhaps he should have remembered something earlier, when, before the War, while we were attending Hebrew school, I threw his new cap into the open latrine. At least for this mischief I got a well-deserved scolding by his father.

I tried to be daring, unafraid, grown-up, and I wanted to help in the household. I took an earthen pitcher from home and went to a neighboring village to buy milk. Poor Iziu attached himself to me. Little did he know that I was apprehensive, too, and did not mind his company. He trudged along, but once we were out of town, he became suspicious. We were in the middle of a meadow. Iziu started crying. He wanted to turn back, to go home; but he was afraid to turn back by himself. We were already too far from town. I felt sorry for him. We made it to the village. I filled the pitcher with milk and got some bread, then walked home with him beside me, crying, pale and scared.

New arrivals gathered into our town, other Jews who were seeking refuge in smaller towns such as Busk. One family came in their very own car. To own a private car was something unheard of, but this one ran out of gas. It found its resting place near the lumberyard in back of our house. Before long, this curiosity, this car, sat completely stripped of its parts and contents. The family was from Bielsko-Biala. They were rumored to have been very wealthy owners of famous woolen mills before the War. The family consisted of a husband and wife, a son my age, an older daughter Tescia, who was very diminutive, a veritable midget, and an elderly grandmother. The family eventually died of cold and starvation in the woods surrounding Busk.

There was another family with a son my age. I mention him because he was so different. He read books. None of my local friends was like him. Eventually I would have been introduced to books and learning. For example, as I have mentioned, my parents purchased a house in Lwów, just prior to the outbreak of the War. The main reason for this was that my parents had plans to provide my brothers and me with an education in Lwów which was unavailable in Busk. But this new boy in town actually read and talked to me about books. He was astonished that I had never heard the names of writers, like Kipling, to mention one. At that time, he was beginning to read Kipling in Ukrainian. He found this hard, because he had to learn the Cyrillic alphabet. His native language was Polish. He thought that I could help him out. After all, he came from the west, from Poland; and I lived in the east, in the Ukraine. He expected me to be fluent in Ukrainian. Little did he know, big city boy that he was, that I did not read any books in any language. He gave me a book in Ukrainian about Indians. It was a struggle to read, but I found it fascinating.

Tescia, the refugee girl from Bielsko-Biala in the west, was older than I. She was very, very small. She had a tiny nose, very small delicate hands and fingers. She manicured her nails, a novelty to me. Her frame was delicate. Everything about her was miniature but in perfect proportion, except for her hair. She had a beautiful crown of long, red hair, always perfectly coiffed. She was a most interesting, intelligent diminutive person. As far as I was concerned, she was grown-up and clever; and I loved to be around her. The family seemed to like me, and I was frequently there. I must admit that she liked me. In fact a conviction grew in me that she wanted me.

The atmosphere grew desperate and many were starving. People were disappearing, sometimes dying of hunger, sometimes being taken away, never to be seen again. Yet people, especially young people, wanted not to miss, or at least to taste, what life could still offer. It happened one afternoon that Tescia and I were alone in the kitchen of her apartment. With trepidation and anxiety we came close to each other. Our faces touched. We kissed hesitantly. Tescia drew me ever so close to her, expectantly. We were dressed;

The Germans

we were anxious; we were ignorant. Bewildered, I found myself on top of her, and just as I was in that confused position, her grandmother burst in from the adjoining room and like a hellish fury itself, gave out a terrible scream. I jumped up and ran out of the house in a panic.

Poor Tescia had sensed, as our other young people sensed, as the grownups sensed, that our lives hung by a thread. If she could, Tescia wanted to have an experience of that mysterious and overwhelming transport which is the culmination of love. But she was not to have it. Our experience may be like hundreds of thousands of experiences my friends might have had, but my friends are gone, their lives snuffed out.

There was a boy of about my age, who appeared on our street. He was all alone. He wore an oversized woolen jacket. Did his father put this jacket on him and tell him to run away, to find some place to hide? This boy was so handsome, so self-assured. He was from some big city. He did not even speak a word of Yiddish. Where did he come from? What happened to him? Was he tortured by some sadistic farmer? Did he die of cold and starvation? Or was he just rounded up in one of the Aktionen with other Jews from a shtetl and joined to them in their fate?

In the early spring of 1942, Ghetto Busk was formed. The Jews from the surrounding villages were herded into the meager and already over-crowded homes of the residents. Even before the Ghetto, the Jews of Busk, as in similar shtetlach, lived in congested, overcrowded and primitive homes or apartments. As a practical matter if not by law, they lived segregated from the Gentile population. Along with the Jewish neighbor-hoods, the buildings in the marketplace, at the center of town, were all Jewish. On the edge of town were the Gentile neighborhoods; further out were the villages, with farmers, mostly Ukrainian, but also Polish.

Then all Jews were made to wear specially made armbands, white with a blue Magen David in the middle. No Jew was allowed to leave the Ghetto except as part of a supervised work crew.

The Germans ordered the formation of a Jewish Committee or Judenrat, as well as a Ghetto police force. These police were issued distinctive blue hats, and also clubs. The Judenrat selected the daily work crews and acted as liaison between the authorities and the Jewish community. The Germans decided how many Jews were to be delivered to them for work at different sites. The Ghetto police then made sure that each household or family complied. Each worker went to the assembly point early in the morning, usually near the Judenrat, and was marched off to an assigned destination.

The Judenrat was located around the corner from Tarnowskiego Street, atop the hill near the place from which I used to start my downhill sledding during the long winters before the Germans came. The members of the Judenrat were feared as much as the police, who were also our own Ghetto Jews. These were the ones who quartered

79

newcomers from the surrounding villages with various of the local Jewish households. The Judenrat could spare one from a work assignment. They could levy a fine on any particular family or, put bluntly, extort a payment in cash or something like jewelry. The Judenrat justified these exactions by pointing to the bribes they needed to pay the authorities. Extortion and bribes were common. At times the whole community was cast into a frenzy when the Judenrat called on it to hand over the gold and valuables the SS demanded in order to suspend an Aktion.

When the SS or some other branch of the Nazis, the ones with the black skull insignia, accompanied by their hired thugs of local militia and fascist volunteers, came to town and herded the Jews into the marketplace; that was an Aktion. They would then take these victims to neighboring woods and kill them. In time, sealed railroad boxcars would take the Jews to their deaths at centralized extermination camps. For the Jews of Busk the death camp, the factory that the Germans built to make death, was in the woods of Belzec.

We sought protection or favors by bribing the Judenrat. Though all Jews of course, they appeared to have some power over the Ghetto. But the truth was, however, that for these members of the Judenrat, the Germans created an illusion of power. While it lasted, the Judenrat officials and the all-Jewish Ghetto police took care of their cronies. They used what power they had, or exploited the powerlessness of those under them, to settle old scores where being Jewish counted for nothing.

Those who became the Ghetto police were usually the local scum. One of our neighbors was especially mean, and he wielded his club without provocation. His name was Laybele. He lived with his very poor mother, had never married, and had no trade. He turned out to be the meanest of all the Ghetto police in Busk. Considering the status of my family and Laybele's low state, I always wondered at his restraint toward us. He could have been a menace. I think that my father bribed him with a pair of boots. Laybele wore his always-shiny boots with the greatest pride.

My mother's aunt Chaya and uncle Mordechai from Lwów moved in with us. So did Jacob and his beautiful young wife Tauba and their one-year-old son Yoynele. Mordechai had been to Boston, Massachusetts, but his wife Chaya had not joined him there because she was terrified of ship travel. He regaled us with stories about America. He had worked as a painter in Boston. He told us about the huge cities, the abundance of food, the immensity of the ocean, the riches of America. In America, he had lived like a millionaire. His wife Chaya became the butt of all our jokes, and his sorrow. Whom else could he blame for now finding himself penniless and starving in Ghetto Busk? Mordechai had returned to Lwów and now found himself and his beloved wife in

Busk. But now he and his Chaya were both on their way to their end, through Ghetto Busk to Belzec, the death camp and the mass grave.

Mordechai suggested we scrape the Polish eagle insignia off the looted silverware we had gotten in that trade with a peasant. This silver really belonged to the Polish government. We all followed his instructions in this enterprise, and the work took many days and nights. Mordechai also built a false fireplace to hide this cache behind.

Later on, after the Judenrein, that is, after Busk had been cleansed of Jews, the local Gentile scavengers demolished our house. Their loot was not just our few remaining possessions. They also took away the wooden beams and sheet-metal roof and scraps of other building materials. To their complete surprise, they found a bonus: the cache of silver in the false fireplace at the back of one of the rooms. But then, some of our local Gentile vultures always suspected that there was gold and silver in Jewish homes. After the War, some enterprising ones dug up the mass graves and extracted gold teeth from the skeletons. When it had been their turn, the Germans had already stolen the victims' rings and other valuables. Exaggerated rumors about what was found in our house survived the War itself.

My mother's stepsister Henia, sixteen years old, came from Lwów to live with us. She was the same age as my oldest brother Chuny. Yoynele, Jacob's and aunt Tauba's son, was just learning how to walk and was a great delight. The front room, which before the War had been the leather-goods store, became additional living space. Many of us had to squeeze in.

We doubled up in bed to sleep. Some slept on the long, scratched-up workbench. Not so long before, this bench had been the main article of furniture in the store.

Once there had been neatly arranged leather goods, separated in bundles. There were soft leather sheets used for shoe uppers, and bundles of hard leather used for soles. All this was further sorted by intended use, gauge, quality, price, etc. Shelves to my father's back held these materials; in front of him was this elongated working bench or counter. This is the bench on which my father would first show samples of leather to his customers. Then they would agree on quality and price. And he would then take expert measurements and lay out the right pattern for size and type of item, and trace its dimensions with white chalk. Finally, he would deftly cut along the lines of the pattern. There was art to how he would bundle up the package of leather and hand it to his customer. I believe that not a piece of leather or even a piece of string was wasted. And I could feel the warmth, the friendship between my father and his customers. They brought countless bundles of fruit as gifts. To this day, when I see a pear, the scene of my father and his customer replays. Together we ate the ripest, sweetest pears the customers had brought. Such moments of the lost past!

The Judenrat assigned to us a family by the name of Flieser, refugees from another town. We all had to fit in together. Eventually, the Fliesers' little girl, then five or six years old, was given away to be hidden by a Gentile family. Miraculously, she survived. It came to pass that after the War, a distant family member of the Fliesers came to enquire about them. My mother helped them trace and reclaim the child, now an orphan. After the Liberation, she emigrated to Israel with her cousin and grew up to be a very handsome woman. She married a doctor in Israel and came to the States several times to visit my mother.

After the War, I noticed that proportionately more newcomers to Busk, those from the western cities, had survived more successfully than had local Jews. We locals were just too complacent, too uncomprehending of our situation. But those who had left their original homes and come to

86

The Germans

Busk were already more experienced, more energized to reach out to prospective sources of help. Also, having already been dispossessed, they had nothing to lose, but they did have strong incentive to venture out and try their luck, despite being among total strangers.

The Judenrat always picked my father and my two brothers for work. I was still at home, but not for long. The time came when the Judenrat picked me, too. This time, I was sent to work for the big German public works agency, Organisation Todt. Our group worked on repairing the main road leading from Lwów to Kiev. I was twelve years old, almost thirteen.

My job was to clean out potholes. Pebbles mixed with tar were thrown in, and a heavy roller then flattened the road surface.

At the work site, several kilometers from Busk, our group met up with another group of Jews from a neighboring town. I worked with my brother Lonek. When with childish pride I pointed him out to some kid from the neighboring town and explained that he was my brother Lonek, I was struck that such an obvious thing needed to be explained. In my naiveté, I assumed that everyone knew my brother Lonek and me.

One day the boiling tar kettle exploded. I was working nearby, and the boiling tar sprayed all over me, particularly onto my exposed face. My face was scorched; my clothes were covered with the black, boiling, clinging tar. There was sudden commotion all around me. I screamed from the pain and shock. Then the German foreman put me in his car and brought me home. It was an odd car. It had three wheels, one in front and two in back. I was allowed to stay home to recover. I had blisters all over my face and body. We all thought that I would have permanent facial marks. But then after some time, my skin peeled and new skin grew, leaving no marks.

The German foreman must have taken a liking to me. As we were driving, he talked to me about socialism, about himself, about things which were completely above my head. Of course, he spoke in German. I could hardly understand him, except for some words, such as "socialism," "communism," "Hitler," "fascism." I grasped that he wanted to convey that he was a working man and against the existing regime. I did not know what to make of this man. Here I was, a Jew, being driven home by a German. What would my neighbors and family think?

Since I did not trust the foreman and did not want him to know where I lived, I pointed out another house in the Ghetto, in front of which he stopped and let me off. Then the foreman told me to take the canister of gasoline he held out to me, a precious commodity in wartime. He assured me that my father would appreciate it and know what to do with it. When I brought the can of gasoline home, my father was very unhappy about it. He was afraid lest this was some kind of trap. He was convinced that the German would come to our house to arrest us on the false charge that we had stolen the gasoline. As it happened, this German meant no harm. On the contrary, in a way he helped to save my immediate family from the Aktion that took place on Yom Kippur, 1942.

Upon my return to work after my injury, the foreman appointed me to be the caretaker of small equipment such as shovels, rakes and brooms; and he gave me the keys to the tool shed, which was like a small railroad car or a caboose.

The day before Yom Kippur there was great anxiety in the town. There were signs of preparation for an Aktion. We were all panic-stricken. I had the keys to the best hiding place. Who would look for Jews on the main road, in a German caboose with the German inscription Org. Todt? My parents, my two brothers and several other members of what remained of our extended family left the Ghetto under cover of darkness. We reached our hiding place, and I unlocked the doors of the caboose. We piled in. It was a very cold

night. At dawn we left and hid all day in the nearby fields. The Jewish road repair crew did not show
up for work that day; and we knew then that there
had been an Aktion, a massacre, and that Jews had
been dragged away from Busk to their deaths.

The following night we all went back home.
During this Yom Kippur Aktion approximately
half of the Jewish population of Busk had been
taken away. We found out later that their destination was Belzec. That is where they were gassed
or shot to death.

We had no answers for what to do. We had to
think of getting the essentials of life: food and
water; and to figure out how to survive the
moment. We were running out of things to barter.
We ran out of soap. We cut up the last pieces of
fences and boards for fuel. I developed boils and
scabs, especially between my fingers. People all
around us were getting sick and dying.

I was awakened one night by a persistent tick-
le around my crotch. I moved my hand to where I

felt it. To my bewilderment I touched a long, slimy, curling thing. I finally pulled from my anus an endless, huge, thick worm.

People placed great hope and trust in God. The more the anxiety, the more the piety. People sighed, "Sy ist schweyer zy zan a Yid," it is hard to be a Jew, with a sense of resignation and acceptance, as if this were pre-ordained. They said, "Der Meschiyach wilt kymen," the Messiah will come. Others would say, "Yes, help will come tomorrow, but we will die today." Still others would live in disbelief, insisting, "Sy ken niszt zan a hefka Welt," the world cannot by ruled by chaos.

The most immediate needs were to find food, to avoid being beaten to death at work, and to elude the typhus. These concerns did not leave us time to search for answers to the reasons for these terrible things happening to us. We had no inner strength left to grasp or invent a way out of our plight.

The Germans

Krasne was one of the sites where Ghetto workers were sent. There we dug ditches and extracted lime. Krasne lay seven kilometers from Busk. It had the railroad station also known as Krasne-Busk. There, a notorious sadist by the name of Januszek ran things. My brother Lonek had been assigned to work there. One day he barely managed to get home, because Januszek had beaten him mercilessly. For the following day's quota I volunteered to stand in for him.

It was still dark when I joined the crew trudging off to the job at Krasne-Busk. Januszek was already waiting to greet his Jews with his shouts and his club. We dug ditches all day to Januszek's shouts and screams and beatings. He was a short young man, blond, with a reddish complexion. He had a violent disposition and was constantly agitated, screaming and hitting someone all the time: "Zyd, Zyd! Macht los! Arbeit! Verfluchter Jude!"

Railroad cars slowly passed loaded with trucks, cannon, military equipment and German soldiers, all heading towards the front in the east. While digging into the lime pit, I would raise my head, despite the danger of Januszek noticing. I was curious to see the cargo and the soldiers. The soldiers appeared like supermen to me. Some were naked to the waist as they washed themselves in the open railroad cars despite the cold autumn weather. This was the autumn of 1942.

It became colder by the day. With the last of our possessions we bartered with peasants for food. There was only one well from which the Ghetto people could fetch their drinking water. Even in the pre-War days there was no indoor plumbing in Busk. There were professional water carriers, but our regular water carrier was slowly giving up his labors. His legs and arms swelled up as a result of the hunger and cold. But he was loyal to his customers to the end. I watched the poor man, who no longer had shoes or boots, as he rolled layers of rags around his feet and legs. Now he walked quietly, carrying the heavy pails filled to the brim with water. A harness hung from his shoulder, a specially carved piece of wood with two pieces of rope hanging from each side. Iron hooks held the handles of two pails of water. But he did not last long after the Ghetto was formed. He died from the cold and starvation.

On cold, wintry days, the walls of the well were packed all around with white and glistening ice. So was the communal bucket attached to its long pole. Thick ice had narrowed the opening to the well. You had to push the long pole with the empty bucket carefully down, then catch the water below. Pulling it up to the top was hard enough; but trickier still was removing the bucket from the hook without spilling, and then pouring the water into your own buckets, while not slipping and falling on the heavy layer of ice that surrounded the well-head.

One day I went to fetch the water. On my way home, I fainted and fell to the side of the road. When I came to, I was already at home. I had been found with a sheet of ice over me, my bucket leaning against me half empty.

The water carrier was one of the first persons to die from the cold and starvation. I witnessed his death. There were more and more of these deaths in the Ghetto. I had once overheard our neighbor the butcher say, "We will never die of starvation." At the time I heard this, I took it to be some ordained law. But even the butcher died of starvation. I lost any trust in such glib remarks.

What was even worse than the cold and starvation was the typhus epidemic. The expression was, people were dying like flies. Several times a day a funeral hurriedly carried the communal bier and shroud down Tarnowskiego Street, and past our house, on its way to the cemetery.

Hanusia was Herman's and aunt Mina's beautiful four-year-old daughter. All children are beautiful, but to me Hanusia was very special: delicate, playful, clever, cuddly, and, indeed, beautiful. She was their only child. Herman and his family were forced to abandon their new home, which was outside the Ghetto boundary, and to relocate to a tiny room just across from our house. Hanusia became ill with typhus. Her blond hair that shone like gold had to be cut off. The poor little child suffered terribly.

When I came to visit her, to hold her hand, she cried; she looked emaciated; she was like a skeleton. I took all this in with a very sad and heavy heart. It took long for Hanusia to get better, and then, even afterward, neither she nor I were ever the same. There was no more playfulness or fun for either of us.

Only months later, Hanusia's mother and father, with Hanusia under his arms, tried to escape to safety. It was on the day of the Judenrein, May 21, 1943. They attempted to swim across the narrow stretch of our river Bug. From positions on the riverbank, the Germans machine-gunned all who tried to get across. That was how they died.

Our river Bug flowed languidly parallel to and just in back of the house where Hanusia and her parents were living. Others tried to escape there with the hope of getting across. They found their end, however, in the same water where I, not so long before, had loved to swim and frolic with other boys and girls and taste the sweetness of life.

Late in 1941, within the first several months of the German occupation, the German SS took truckloads of Jews to neighboring woods. There, the Germans forced them to dig large ditches, then shot them to death so that they would fall in. Executions like this happened before trains of freight cars began to take Jews to work camps, the name used for extermination camps. My beloved grandparents were among those first victims.

In fact, and perhaps curiously so, there was no pogrom in Busk, though one was expected at the beginning of the German occupation. We expected drunken Cossacks, Ukrainians, Germans and their henchmen to ride into town brandishing sabers, shooting their guns off indiscriminately, killing the Jews and burning and maiming the terrified, the bleeding, the screaming and the dying. But we did not have a pogrom, and I began to believe that my Busk was special, that my Busk was different, that nothing bad could happen to us Jews in Busk.

But the actual slaughter was better organized and more modern than that. Besides the local Ukrainian militia, German soldiers, special SS troops and additional Ukrainian militiamen from other places came into our town. They went from home to home to fill their quota of victims and bring them to the gathering point in the rynek. There they shoved them onto trucks, drove away to the outskirts of the city, and shot them dead. Finished! In a later phase, the victims were brought to the Krasne railroad station to be transported to death camps. The monstrous word for this, in the context of that time and those events, was Aktion, newer and sleeker than the old-fashioned and much less lethal Pogrom.

Life Death Memories

Later I learned, to my amazement, that it was the Metropolitan Andrei Sheptytsky, of the Ukrainian Orthodox Church diocese of Lwów who signaled his parishioners not to conduct pogroms. This indeed was almost like a miracle, as historically the Church was one of the main sources of anti-Semitism. Without the intervention of this noble person, the followers of Petliura and Bandera would have been the first to maim, kill and decimate our Jewish communities. These Ukrainian nationalist organizations were allied with the Germans, who had promised the Ukrainians an independent Ukraine, where historically they had been subjugated by the mighty Russians. Because the Jewish minority had accommodated itself to the prevailing regimes, the Nationalists saw this attitude of the Jews as contrary to their own interests, and thus an additional reason, besides what the Church taught them, to hate the Jews.

100

The Germans

They blamed the Jews for their land being occupied first by Polish and then Russian governments. They accused the Jews of being communists or capitalists, depending on circumstances. And, of course, they accused the Jews of being the killers of Jesus Christ. According to the Gospel of the Ukrainians and the Poles, the Jews were to blame for all that was bad: the poverty, the wars, the calamities; and with the Jews gone, their salvation would come. Besides hatred, there was greed: an instant reward for killing the Jews was helping oneself to their property. Victimizing this minority thus served the purposes of the Czars, the Nationalists, Polish or Ukrainian, the racists and the Church authorities, too. After all, someone had to be blamed for the evils of the world. To them it was the Jews.

Yet, even in the worst of times, I was still to be made a full-fledged member of the Jewish tribe. My bar mitzvah was approaching. My parents asked our next-door neighbor, a very poor, respectable, religious man, to teach me the prayers and how to put on the phylacteries. At dawn on November 27, 1942, my thirteenth birthday, before assembling for the work crew near the Judenrat, several men gathered to form a minyan to say the morning prayers and celebrate with my family my becoming a full member of the Jewish community. My mother prepared some refreshments for the men who came. It was against the law to gather for a minyan or in fact to gather for any social or religious function. My bar mitzvah was kept a secret. It was held at an unfinished corner of a neighbor's house.

I did not use the phylacteries for long. As for praying, I prayed intensely, passionately, secretively, making up my own prayers to God. Somehow, I had the conviction that I had a special protection from and intimate relationship with God. Even before the War, when I was on my way to school, I would avoid everyone so that I could pray. I fervently beseeched God to help me, to be my family's protector. In my naiveté and my belief in the all-powerful, I also asked for His help to make me understand arithmetic and to protect us from anti-Semitic deeds, such as stones thrown at windows. Later, I prayed that my father not be deported to Siberia and asked for God's intervention in similar very personal affairs. To my eternal shame, I even entreated God, when I was especially angry or slighted, to punish my older brother Chuny. At times I also had visions of a mystical or religious nature. One recurring vision was of a candelabra ascending from me and carrying my prayers directly to heaven.

There came a time when the Judenrat was told to organize a small, select group of able-bodied young men. They would be given a special badge and have special privileges. They would live outside the Ghetto and be assigned special jobs. They would be safe. To get into this special work group, one had to have a connection in the Judenrat. Using some influence, my brother Chuny gained admission to it. My mother fitted him out with whatever better clothes we still had, and he moved out of the house to live with the special work group on the outside.

The long, cold winter of 1942-1943 set in. A Polish entrepreneur from the city of Lwów came to Busk and put up a notice that he had been assigned to take identification photos of the Ghetto residents. The price for the photos was exorbitant, but he said they were mandatory. He set up his camera on a tripod on top of the Tarnowskiego Street hill, near the Judenrat, ready for business. The Ghetto population was by now so physically and mentally exhausted that we would have fallen for any lie or scheme. It turned out that the photographer was a fraud who came to town only to extort money from the Jews.

One day, to my enormous surprise, a Ukrainian friend from boyhood sought me out in the Ghetto. He took a risk for this visit, for no one was allowed to enter the Ghetto without permission. He was a friend from the time we had been in school together. I was embarrassed to see him. It was only two years since we had been school-mates, but it felt as though I had known him an eternity ago and in a different world. He said that he was about to join the Bandera volunteers, which meant fighting with the Germans against the Russians.

Even though the Petliura and Bandera people, all Ukrainian Nationalists, did not conduct a pogrom of their own against the Jews of Busk, they enlisted in the local militias and helped the Germans in the Aktionen, in the annihilation of the Jews. In addition, there was the Vlasov army of nationalist Ukrainian Cossacks, most of whom had defected from the Russian Red Army and joined the Germans to fight against the Russians, because they had been promised an independent Ukraine. They were a scourge of the Jews. They were as cruel as the Germans.

Life Death Memories

The Ukrainian boy came to see me bringing with him a hunting knife as a gift. He told me to keep it and defend myself with it. He knew, of course, that Jews were being killed. I hid the knife on a beam in the shed in back of our house. Every so often I would go to look at it and hold it in my hands without a thought about what to use it for. I noticed that the handle was getting loose, that it was shrinking. I realized that it needed moisture. I placed the handle in a cup filled with water and, indeed, the handle expanded and became tight. My father would have been shocked to find out about this weapon and my secret activity.

We had no radios or newspapers. We were entirely dependent upon rumors for any sense of the events of the War and especially about what was happening on the eastern front. We gathered that the War was going poorly for our oppressors. But resignation was setting in, hope was fading; and our mood was best expressed like this: "The liberation will come next week, but we will die tomorrow."

We knew that some families were frantically searching for ways to get out of the Ghetto, looking for a hiding place. Our family decided to stay together. Men and boys had nowhere to go because we were circumcised. I fantasized about doing something to hide that circumcision, but this was never more than a fantasy. We would be detected, discovered, caught and killed. Better to be together.

Our fate seemed clear and inescapable. Our people were being put to death. We were being exterminated. There was no longer any doubt about it. Still, we did not know just how; we did not know about the gas chambers.

Rumors reached us of Jews being taken away from other shtetlach to camps in railway freight cars. We had no clear idea of death camps, or death factories. We children were told, however, to try to escape from the cars. We were told to try to jump out, and always to jump forward, in the direction of the train's movement. Then, once on the ground, we were told, we should stretch out flat in the ditch adjacent to the railroad tracks to avoid the anticipated gunfire from the German guards.

I would imagine myself lying in a ditch after a successful jump, with bullets flying from the guards, and the speeding train leaving me behind. The thought was terrifying and exciting: I could still imagine adventure. Remember, we were told, never to jump in the opposite direction of the speeding train.

We were also told that, before going to sleep, we should keep clothes and shoes near our bed so that we could get dressed at once if an Aktion began in the dark and we should need to run to our hiding places. These were our only lessons in survival!

For women or girls, especially the less observant, the attempt to pass as an Aryan was easier. A few young girls were able to obtain false Aryan papers with the help of Polish or Ukrainian peasants and using them they went on trains to Germany, with shipments of Aryan peasants bound for farm or factory work in Germany. My mother obtained false papers through Mrs. Fedorska for my mother's half-sister Henia. Just in time, Henia joined a train to Germany carrying Aryan men and women. She survived the War.

Die Aktion

It was Friday, May 21, 1943. At dawn the Ghetto was surrounded. The final Aktion in Ghetto Busk began. Busk was to become Judenrein, cleansed of its Jews.

We had two hiding places, or schrons, in our house. Schron was the Polish word for hiding place or shelter. One schron was in the room at the back of our house where, during the Russian occupation, the mining engineer had lived with his local woman. That was the room where uncle Mordechai, the one who had lived in Boston, had built a false fireplace. In this room we dug out a small cave, almost like a small cellar under the floor, with a trap door made out of the floorboards.

Another schron was in the attic, in the space between the gable-end of the house and a false wall which had been built behind two roof-beams.

We awakened to shouts and screams and crying and gunfire. "Gewalt! Gewalt!", a cry for help in Yiddish. Then German: "Macht los! Verfluchter Jude! Heraus, Jude, heraus!" With his one-year-old son Yoynele, Jacob ran to the backroom schron. Uncle Mordechai and his wife went there too, along with the young Flieser couple. They had placed their toddler with a Polish family. As mentioned before, the child survived the War. In panic and in total darkness, my father, my mother, my brother Lonek, aunt Tauba, Jacob's wife and I ran up to the attic schron.

We stayed there for several days. During the first day we heard women and children wailing. All day, blaring curses in German and volleys of gunfire filled the street. There was nothing but chaos. In mid-morning the doors to our house were smashed open. The Germans and their Ukrainian thugs discovered the back-room shelter. The family members hiding there were dragged off to the marketplace.

I never found out what happened. Had Yoynele started crying for his mother Tauba, who was in our group in the attic schron? Did Yoynele need to be fed? Or had he just started to cry because of the terrible noise and chaos? Or did Mordechai cough? He must have been suffocating in that hole in the ground. How did the killers find the schron? I will never know. The murderers were at least clever enough to know that people were hiding.

Years after, though I had many chances, I did not have the courage to speak to Jacob about how they were delivered to the marketplace on that hellish day. The Jews driven out of their homes or hiding places were all brought to the rynek and surrounded by the German SS and the

Ukrainian militias. Empty German trucks were lined up waiting.

Itzchak, the philosopher, who, in his naiveté, had written the famed letter of greetings that he made me deliver to the German officer, failed to go into the hiding place. Neither did Mr. Weissblitt go into a schron. He had stayed in our house off and on. He was the pre-War owner of sawmills and an exporter of lumber to the west, the richest man in and around Busk. He hanged himself.

The schron in the attic was never found.

In the days that followed we heard sporadic cries and shots from the street. The cries for help and prayers were from people being dragged out of their hiding places as the militias and the Germans took them off to the local prison or directly to the Jewish cemetery.

I found out later from Jacob, or was it his brother Tulu, some additional details about May 21, 1943, and the days shortly thereafter. First about little Yoynele. Then about my brother Chuny.

114

Die Aktion

By May 21, 1943, those remaining of the Jews
of Busk who were rounded up were dragged to the
rynek. Once there, they were ordered to sit down.
Then the German SS proceeded to make a selec-
tion. They segregated young, able-bodied men on
one side, and older or frail-looking men, as well as
women and children, on the other side. While
Jacob was holding Yoynele in his arms, Tauba's
mother, the baby's grandmother, came over. She
implored Jacob to give Yoynele to her. She took
the crying child from Jacob's arms. We never
heard of Yoynele or his grandmother again. Nor
was Yoynele's name, or what happened on that
day, May 21, 1943, ever mentioned in Jacob's or
Tauba's presence. To this very day, I do not have
the courage to talk to Tauba about Yoynele.

Tulu's wife Salka, Mr. Weissblitt's daughter,
was a young physician, who had attended medical
school in Vienna. She spoke German fluently. In
the chaos at the rynek, she pushed herself forward
to a German officer. She introduced herself as a

physician. She offered her professional services in caring for the crying children and the hysterical and fainting people. She pointed to the wailing, panic-stricken children around her, and she assured the officer that she could calm them and be of help. The officer hit her and ordered her to sit down on the ground like all the others and not move. This is the last we heard of Salka, the healer, the just-licensed physician, and her six-year old daughter Ruth.

Ruth was Tulu and Salka's only child. Of course, to all parents, their little children are genius level, if not exceptional. From the time Ruth and her parents came from Lwów to find safety in Busk, in their deference towards their daughter, and even in their reserve towards us, they had convinced us that their Ruth was a genius, certainly something special. Ruth, they called her Ruthie, spoke Polish and German fluently. She was the most doted-upon child; no one in Busk paid such attention to a child. But Ruth, who was always meticulously dressed, was talked about and held in awe. Not only was she the child of a doctor, but the grandchild of Mr. Weissblitt, the richest man in and around Busk. Ruth was indeed different from us. She was a little aristocrat. She never fit in with the other children. Only in her ultimate fate did she join them fully.

Towards the end of the day, on May 21, 1943, the Jews who were assembled in the rynek were herded into the waiting trucks and brought to the Krasne station. There, railway cattle-cars were ready for them. It was all neatly coordinated. The Jews from Busk and surrounding shtetlach were then locked into the cars and sent onward under guard to the Belzec death camp. Yes, that was their destination: hell on earth. And the train puffed along, even making some innocent local stops. The planning was detailed. The Germans picked up Jews from still other shtetlach here and there as the train continued on its way to Belzec.

Several truckloads of Jewish men were not taken to the Krasne station. They were delivered instead to the Janowska labor camp, outside of Lwów.

This is what happened to my oldest brother Chuny. Jacob and Tulu were put with the able-bodied men in the Janowska camp. This camp, though known as a labor camp, was really a camp of extermination without gas chambers. Upon their arrival, the victims were ordered to hand over any rings, coins, jewelry, watches, anything of value. Then they were assigned to their various groups and barracks. There, Jacob met up again with Chuny, who had been permitted to live outside our Ghetto because of being in a so-called special work group. The Germans quartered this group in a few houses on the edge of our Ghetto vacated when their owners were relocated inside it.

But this was surely a German plan of deception to segregate young able-bodied men from the general population by seeming to offer them protection. Parents would be happy in the vain hope that at least their son would survive. The men were assured they would be considered a protected group needed for essential tasks. But this protected work group living outside the Ghetto was in fact among the first to be taken to the rynek. Among them was my older brother Chuny, sixteen years of age.

When he arrived at the Janowska camp he wore only a pair of sandals. As Jacob recounted it later, all newly arrived inmates were gathered together at a central area, the Appelplatz, to receive instructions. In this assembly place there was a heap of shoes, boots and clothing. The German officer yelled out orders and warnings. The prisoners had to surrender any and all of their valuables, and were warned that failure to do so would result in death. Then they were told that they could select for themselves shoes or boots or clothing from the heap in front of them.

My brother Chuny took a pair of shoes from the pile. He put them on in place of his sandals. Then the guard came over and ordered him to take off the shoes. This he did. The guard then examined the shoes and claimed he had found a gold coin hidden inside. My brother protested that he knew nothing about it. The guard started to beat my Chuny mercilessly over the head, making an example of him as a warning to the rest not to try to hide valuables. Then the guard plunged his finger into Chuny's eye and gouged it out.

Who will ever know if the German planted the evidence, or if he even needed a pretext for his sadistic act of cruelty? My brother and all the rest of the inmates, were not only emaciated, but harmless and utterly powerless. Even so, the guard resorted to tricks to terrorize his victims about concealing anything.

Jacob was a man of few words. He was deliberate, hesitant, and visibly in pain as he described my brother's agony, as well as his own rage and powerlessness. His glance downcast, his voice barely audible and his lips quivering, he told what had happened to Chuny. Had he, Jacob, done anything to protest or resist, as was his impulse, the machine guns nearby were ready to cut him apart along with the others. My blinded brother Chuny did not survive.

Several days passed. Jacob and his brother Tulu were making plans to escape from Janowska. This with the knowledge that in retaliation, the Germans would shoot many prisoners for each of those who succeeded in escaping or could not be accounted for. Of course, eventually they killed everyone anyway. But by tricking and dehumanizing, the Germans made use of the victims' growing belief that by being obedient, submissive, almost invisible, they would overcome and survive. What would a person not do, if he had to choose between surviving and dying! Having only this choice, a person is stripped of his human qualities. The Germans' manipulations, the prisoners' exhaustion, their powerlessness, the dogs, the armed guards who were everywhere during the daytime and on the towers with floodlights at night, as well as the retaliation against others, instilled an inertia, a paralysis, that stifled most escape attempts, let alone resistance. Despite it all, Jacob and Tulu decided to try.

First, they tried frantically to find my brother Chuny and take him with them. He was nowhere to be found. And so the two, Jacob and Tulu, and possibly another, crawled in the darkness to the barbed wire, cut out an opening, and successfully made their escape.

In the meantime, we were still in our schron in the attic. We also were preparing to make our own breakout. It was becoming unbearable to stay in the schron any longer. During the day we were as quiet as the dead. The strong sun heated up the sheet metal roof just above our heads and baked us. In the evenings and especially overnight it grew very cold. It was then that my father or I crawled stealthily downstairs in total darkness to search for some water and crumbs of food. We also had to dispose of our bodily waste. That meant crossing the street and walking over to the river with a full pail and dumping it quietly into the water. We were constantly aware that the street and the riverbanks were still being closely watched. In the house, nothing was as it had been. The rooms had been ransacked. Whatever household items were left were strewn everywhere. When awakened to run and hide, Lonek had climbed up to the attic schron with only his shorts on and no shoes. The following night he found his shoes and some clothes. I was fully dressed. I had gone to sleep the night before the Aktion remembering to be prepared just in case.

We began to run out of water, and even of crumbs of food. The alternating heat and cold became more than we could stand. We knew that, by day, continuous house-to-house searches were being made. The oppressors expected to uncover still more hiding Jews. Additionally, work crews were beginning to circulate looking for anything to remove from the deserted homes. So we knew that we would eventually be found.

There was no choice but to leave the schron, with some dim hope of salvation, of some help, outside. We decided that the family must split up. I chose to leave with my mother and Tauba as the first group. Lonek was to leave the following night with our father.

My parents knew a kind lady, Mrs. Dawidowska, who lived near the Jewish cemetery, at whose place we were to meet up, if the escapes worked.

Escape

We parted as darkness fell. Mother, Tauba and I crawled out of the schron and carefully and quietly left the house. We finally succeeded in getting out of the Ghetto area. But in a meadow just beyond, we came under gunfire. Bullets whistled past my ear. We ran. We ran towards a grove. I was falling exhausted behind my mother and Tauba. But she would not let go of me. As I ran, I prayed silently. I prayed: bullet, bullet, kind bullet, strike me, please, let me feel your searing heat on my skin! Please, strike me, kind bullet; please let me die!

Life Death Memories

We reached the trees and fell down to catch our breath; and again all grew quiet.

We went through meadows, then another grove, and passed by our Jewish cemetery. I knew that I was leaving forever many a friend and neighbor lying in new graves in puddles of their own blood.

Those not caught in the Aktion of May 21, 1943 and taken away by train to Belzec or by truck to Janowska and who had not been killed right on the streets of Busk were brought to our Jewish cemetery to be killed there and left in common graves. Only a few men were left to do the cleanup work in the Ghetto.

This is what happened to our dentist's daughter. This young girl, sixteen or seventeen years old, was too embarrassed to undress before her executioners, as she was ordered to do. She was then beaten up and her clothes torn off. Only then, as she stood stark naked, was she shot and then fell into the pit. She is so often on my mind.

Escape

That even in these desperate circumstances she was embarrassed to be seen naked by strange men is paradoxical. Strange. Death is at hand, yet this human quality remains, of being shy and embarrassed. Did she not understand? Did shyness hide death from her? Was her pain and fright any less?

This girl, the daughter of the town's only dentist, was an enigma to me from the time she and her family came to live in Busk. They settled in our town just before the War. He was the only dentist. There were two daughters. The one I remember most was pale, with long black hair. To me, she seemed unapproachable, always looking so unhappy and so melancholy. Of course, I was younger and should not have expected to become her friend. She was much more sophisticated than the other girls of Busk. Did she miss her friends? Was she some romantic dreamer whose head was in the clouds? Or was she simply lonely and unable to make friends in our small town? This was before the War and before the Russian occupation. She was so delicate, so pale, so unhappy and so alone. Who could have imagined that this frail creature could resist anything? Yet she did. She refused to undress obediently before falling into her eternal sleep.

We finally found our way to Mrs. Dawidowska's, whose tiny farm was close to the Jewish cemetery. She was a poor farmer's widow, with a young daughter. But she was kind. The daughter had a speech impediment and could hardly form a sentence. Mrs. Dawidowska was panic-stricken when we woke her up in the middle of the night. She knew what was going on. Though deathly scared, she did not turn us away.

She was afraid her neighbors might turn her in for having anything to do with Jews. So she led us to her field and told us to lie still and stay hidden among the wheat stalks. She brought us food. After several days, we still had no sign from Lonek and our father. They were to have contacted us through Mrs. Dawidowska.

Escape

Soon enough she knew she could not help us any longer. Her fields were too small and too close to her unreliable neighbors. And she could not hide and feed three people. Above all, she was scared to death. Living so near to our Jewish cemetery, she must have heard frequent blasts of gunfire.

So we left Mrs. Dawidowska's and trudged in darkness through outlying fields, groves and forests, my mother, Tauba and I, heading nowhere in particular. During the day we lay low, hiding stretched out between stalks of wheat or corn. Later on, after the harvest, we hid in groves covered by potato, radish or beet leaves. And while we lived in the fields, we ate raw corn, wheat grains, roots, radishes, beets and berries. Water came from streams or even puddles.

Peasants worked in their fields. Emboldened by hunger, I would approach field workers, beg for food or something to drink and offer to work. Then I would bring to my mother and Tauba whatever I had scrounged.

131

On one of my expeditions for food, I approached a group of women working in the field. One of the women, who appeared to be the boss or maybe the owner, at first seemed amused at my offer to help with their work. With clear sarcasm, she said she could see I was not a farm boy, and that my poor, delicate hands would get bruised from the thorns and weeds, and that I wouldn't be able to stand it. I felt challenged but inspired. On the spot I composed and declaimed a verse in fluent Ukrainian. It went like this: "The pain within from hunger exceeds the pain without from boils, and your reward for kindness will outweigh what you get for your toils." The woman was pleased with my performance and allowed me to stay. But I guess I was not much help, not knowing which weeds to pull up and which plants to leave alone. Soon she had second thoughts about me, too.

After a short while she gave me a black earthenware pitcher of milk and a loaf of bread, and told me I should go on my way, that it was dangerous for me to be there. I could keep the pitcher. With my treasure, I took leave of the peasant farmers. A pitcher, an ordinary pitcher! What a precious item this is. Just stop for a second and think about it. With this, we could now store water or milk, when we were lucky enough to get some. The pitcher was to be a great possession. I was elated over having met the farm workers.

A day or two later, with the black pitcher in hand, I went into a village hoping that someone would have mercy and give me some bread and milk. My hair was dark blond. I was not a particularly Semitic-looking boy, though, against the homogeneous Ukrainian and Polish population, one could easily distinguish anyone's ethnic make-up. But we were starving, and someone had to get food, milk or water. It was time to try my luck. Among the three of us I was the least recognizable as Jewish, and I insisted on going to the village during the day.

Life Death Memories

While trudging off to the village in full daylight, I kept looking back to fix in my mind land-
marks for the place in the field where my mother
and Tauba remained hidden. I was near the village square when a young boy came over to me.
He asked me where I was going. I told him I had
come to look for milk and bread. He said, "Come
along with me." As I followed him, nearing the
house where he promised I could get some, I
noticed two bicycles leaning against the wall. The
sight electrified me with an instinctive jolt of suspicion. Swiftly, like an animal, I turned around
and ran toward the fields. The young village boy
turned and ran after me. Just then, two Ukrainian
militiamen bolted out of the house, and they, too,
chased me. It was a trap. I was caught and
brought back to where the bicycles were leaning
against the wall.

Now I knew I was facing my end. I started to
scream and cry hysterically. I implored them in
Ukrainian to spare me, to let me go, to let me live.

Escape

I begged them. I hung onto their sleeves. I swore that I had done no wrong. I prayed: I wanted to live. I trembled and shivered like a fish on a hook. I turned my head and clasped my hands toward heaven and beseeched God, as loud as I could, "Please let me live!" My voice and words started to fail me. Tears and sweat were all over my face. No, I did not want to be taken to Busk, to the cemetery. "Please, good, compassionate people, let me live!"

Villagers began gathering at the scene. In the meantime, they had called for a horse-drawn cart to come and drive me to Busk, to deliver me to the executioners. The militiamen told me that they knew there were Jews hiding in the fields. They promised me that if I led them to the hiding places of the other Jews, they would let me go. I insisted that there were no other Jews, that I was all alone. Then there was a commotion among the villagers who had gathered to watch. A woman, a hunchback, ran out from her house and joined the crowd. She was very agitated. She pushed herself up close to look at me. Then she turned on the militiamen and in a loud and accusatory voice started screaming at them. She quoted the Bible. She threatened that punishment and damnation in hell would be meted out to them for wanting to kill an innocent boy. In her passionate and religious fervor, she derided the strong and armed militiamen. She commanded them to let me go, or else! But all to no avail.

The cart was approaching that they had requisitioned to take me to Busk. The hunchbacked woman now turned to me and urged me to run away. Quivering, frightened and exhausted, drained by now even of my tears, I gasped, "They will shoot me in the back!" She said, "Run! They will not dare shoot you." I pushed my way through the crowd and ran for my life. The militiamen ran after me. They caught me again on the edge of the village square. Again they promised not to take me away if I led them to the hiding place of the other Jews. Again, in total exhaustion, I cried and begged and assured them that I was all alone. This time, a smaller crowd had followed along, with my savior, the hunchback, in the lead. I was let go. I turned around and ran, expecting to feel a bullet strike me in the back.

After I ran into the fields in a zig-zag pattern to make sure I was not being followed, I rejoined my mother and Tauba, who had been in their hiding place anxiously waiting for me. They had heard some of the crying and commotion and had thought the worst. We waited till evening. Then we left the field and headed to the nearby woods.

We reached a beautiful pine forest. Our hope now was to hide there, and possibly find someone to help us.

While we were hiding in the forest, a villager found us. He meant us no harm, because he knew who we were. He told us that my father and brother had been caught. They had been brought to our Jewish cemetery and there they were shot and killed. Hearing this, I grew numb. I walked away from the others and farther into the woods, to be alone, to absorb the shock.

Then I felt some type of relief, like a sudden enlightenment. I thought: the worst has just happened to me, and yet I survived. The worst grief and pain can occur only once. My own death will be a reunion with my two most beloved people, my father and my Lonek. I would not have to undergo such a shock or loss ever again. The pain and shock of having lost my most beloved father and my most beloved brother Lonek would always be more than any future loss or pain.

I was struck also with the thought that it was all right for me to hate God. During this epiphany, I vowed never to fast on Yom Kippur, as a sign of defiance of God. At the same time I vowed never to say the Kaddish for my father and Lonek. This is the obligatory solemn prayer recited for the dead, which is, at the same time, a hymn in praise of God.

Escape

After a day or two in the woods, we walked in what we thought was the direction of the forester's house. My mother had some notion that the forester would know of Jewish people or even Russian or Jewish partisans hiding there and that he would connect us with them, or better, that perhaps the forester would be inclined to help us. After several attempts to find him, we finally located his house, and then the forester himself. He wore an impressive uniform and had a rifle slung over his shoulder. He indicated that he understood our situation and our need. He appeared to be sympathetic. Tauba gave him a gold watch, a treasure that she had sewn into an undergarment. I found out about the watch from Tauba only recently.

The forester told us to go into the woods and stay by the trail, and he would meet us there for a talk. I had an eerie feeling looking at this man. Tauba told me many years later that she, too, was struck by the forester's facial expression. "His face changed. It started suddenly to look like an animal's when he grabbed the watch."

While waiting for the forester to meet us, as he had instructed, I felt engulfed by fear. I had a sudden premonition that he would be coming to kill us. In a fit of anxiety I cried out that we must run away, that we must hide immediately. But my mother brushed me off and urged us to stay, believing that the man would help us. In an uncontrollable rage, I grabbed our most precious possession, the black earthen pitcher, and, like a Moses, lifted it up and threatened to smash it to the ground unless we ran away. My mother was petrified. She relented.

In years to come she would remind me of this scene. Tauba also recalled that I cried, "I want to live! I want to live! I don't want to die! We must run away!" And that is what we did.

From a distance, afterward, we saw the forester, like the hunter he was, approaching with his rifle, looking for us. We were in nearby fields, but he was looking for us among the trees and bushes. Next day, in a steady downpour, we lay in the fields near the forest and saw several Ukrainian militiamen, led by the forester, come striding by with their carbines slung upside down over their shoulders. Soon enough we heard gunshots coming from the forest. We later learned that the forester would first pretend to give advice and help. Then he would rob his victims, lost, helpless, hunted Jews. Such an arrangement! The forester, the predator in disguise, enjoyed the convenience of seeing his prey come right up to him seeking help.

While we suffered our trials in the forest, Jacob and Tulu, at the Janowska camp, had succeeded in cutting an opening in the wire fence one night and bolting away. We knew nothing of this. Without them, my mother's, Tauba's and my fate would have been sealed. I was getting to be utterly tired and resigned. In fact, I had had enough. I wanted to die. The hunger pains, the thirst and, above all, the loneliness became unbearable. I begged my mother to let me go. I wanted to die in the company of other people, among the remaining Jews of Busk. Death was becoming inevitable and enviable. How much easier, I thought, would it be to die in the company of others.

My mother in her fierce determination kept me from giving myself up or from running away. I had obeyed, for I started to have a feeling of obligation towards her now that my father was gone. I recall now another occasion, in the winter of 1943-1944, when my mother woke me to ask if I could feel my toes. I said, "No," and told her to leave me alone and let me sleep. But she immediately pulled off my icy shoes and found my feet frozen and lifeless. She rubbed them with snow until some blood and feeling came back. Had she not thought that my feet were freezing, would I have become a cripple? It was an example of her unwavering concern for me.

Escape

As we were wandering in the fields, scavenging for food, a Ukrainian peasant, whose name we later learned was Mrs. Smaha, was in her fields along with her workers. She noticed us, thinking that she recognized Tauba. She approached us and spoke to Tauba. Then she suggested that we remain in hiding close by. She said she would return to us after milking the cows. Indeed, she did return with milk and bread. She pointed out her house, the only one in the village with a red tiled roof. She told us that at night we should move closer to her house, to a place she showed us. She promised to bring us food and to talk to her husband about helping us.

We drew near her house during the night and settled in her fields as she had indicated. For several days Mrs. Smaha came to see us and brought us food and drink. She herself was frightened at her conspiratorial activity. After all, the penalty was death for the entire families of those caught helping Jews. The Smahas were among the most

143

prominent people in their village. Mr. Smaha was an active member of the local Ukrainian Nationalist faction. Most of the Ukrainian organizations were pro-Nazi. What they all had in common was their virulent and traditional anti-Semitism. Most of them actively assisted the Germans in their enterprise of exterminating Jews. But there were exceptions.

One evening Mrs. Smaha came over to our hiding place and asked Tauba to come with her to her house. She said that her husband had come back from a trip and wanted to meet her and have a talk with her. Tauba followed, not knowing what to expect. When she met Mr. Smaha, Tauba told about herself and that Jacob was her husband and that he worked in the lumber business. Mr. Smaha recalled that before the War he had worked at the sawmill for Mr. Weissblitt, the owner, and that Mr. Smaha's neighbor, Mr. Komendiuk, also Ukrainian, was Jacob's school friend. Further, Mr. Komendiuk had worked with the manager of the

Escape

Ukrainian cooperative in Busk, a Mr. Turkiewicz, with whom Jacob had worked during the Russian occupation and right up to the liquidation of the Ghetto, until he, Jacob, was taken away to the Janowska camp on May 21, 1943.

Mr. Smaha suggested that Tauba write a letter to Mr. Turkiewicz asking for help or at least information about her husband or her family. Tauba did so. It went to Mr. Komendiuk, who gave it to Mr. Turkiewicz in Busk.

Eventually, after escaping from Janowska, Jacob and Tulu hiked through fields and woods from Lwów to the vicinity of Busk. They were starving. They hid during daylight in strange barns and fields, frightened, hunted and exhausted. Finally they reached their uncertain destination. Among other former trusted friends, they approached Mrs. Dawidowska. Jacob asked Mrs. Dawidowska if she would contact Mr. Turkiewicz, who had been his best friend. As Mrs. Dawidowska did so, Mr. Turkiewicz had just then received Tauba's letter. He in turn got back to Mr. Komendiuk, who told the Smahas.

None of this was simple to do. After all, Mr. Turkiewicz and Mr. Komendiuk were part of the Ukrainian administration of Busk and active Nationalists. There were enemies everywhere. Even those exceptional people who wanted to be of help had to watch out for their own skins.

Mrs. Smaha came to our hiding place. She looked harried and agitated as she turned to Tauba asking her not to scream out. "What, the War is over!" "No," said Mrs. Smaha, "but your husband is alive; he escaped with his brother. We will help you get together."

In the meantime, Mrs. Dawidowska gave Jacob and Tulu food and shelter in her field.

One night, the Smahas asked us to come into their barn. There, Jacob and Tulu, almost unrecognizable, appeared before us. Now we felt less forlorn. There were two grown men with us. It was then that we learned what had happened to Chuny at Janowska.

My preoccupations at the time were chiefly to suppress my hunger and thirst and to remain undetected and thus, hopefully, to survive. But the scene of Chuny's torment haunted me. And I had a nagging feeling of shame concerning him. Had God listened to my prayers when I lay in bed in our home and begged God to punish Chuny, to destroy him? After all, I prayed so fervently and so often and had such evil wishes. Should I not have been punished instead for the evil thoughts? But it was my older, bigger, clever brother who had been tortured and killed! Was there any explanation for all this?

Fall was approaching. The cold, pouring rains were setting in. The tall stalks of wheat and corn were gone, and so we no longer had that kind of camouflage. Now the hiding places in the fields were among the furrows between the rows of potatoes, beets and radishes. We had to lie stretched out immobile all the daylight hours covered by plant leaves or deep in the muddy furrows. The sticky mud, the cold, the danger all about were unbearable. And then, as the potatoes became ready for harvest, the farmers would arrive to dig them up. The fields were becoming barren, with no foliage left to use for cover. And the incessant cold rain or monotonous cold drizzle, and the wet, black mud in which we lay immersed day and night drove me to utter despair. It was too cold to remove my wet rags to look for the lice that were biting me. For distraction, I turned everything I did, whether digging out a potato or a weed, or killing a louse, into pretending I was killing a German whom I'd caught.

I wanted to die. Yet, I also wanted revenge on the Germans for taking away my beloved father and my beloved brothers. Time and again I could imagine my oldest brother standing there alone, forlorn, with tears and blood streaming down his face, shrieking in bewilderment and despair, "Why did you blind me?"

We wore the same clothes, now in rags, in which we had escaped from the schron. We had no soap. Only the rainwater cleansed the mud and dirt from our bodies. Later, in the winter, we washed ourselves with snow. We were infested with lice. Again and again, when I plucked a louse from my body or hair or one of the rags covering me, and when I squeezed it, making a stream of my own blood run out, I fantasized that I was killing Germans; and there was some consolation in that.

Despite all, there were periods when I had imaginings of better times to come. A recurring daydream was that I led my mother up a long, wide staircase to a palace. I imagined a warm land. I dreamed of running away to Hungary, from there to Turkey, and then to a promised land known in those days as Palestine. My desires fluctuated: I wanted to die, and then I wanted to live.

And so, when I was in a more hopeful state of mind, I still prayed to God to let me live. I made all kinds of promises to God and begged Him to help us, to save us. I vowed never to complain about my lot if only I were to live, and that I would be fully satisfied if I were to live just long enough to hear of the death of Hitler. I bargained with God that if I were to survive, I would be grateful and satisfied if I had nothing more than the cheapest and most basic foods, like mamalyga, corn meal, which I had hated as a child. At other times, I prayed, I implored, that God allow me to live so that at least once, just once, I could make love to a woman.

The time came when the Smahas told us that they could not continue to help us. The village was full of Ukrainian Nationalists, both Banderas and Petliuras. Most of them were haters and murderers of Jews. Jacob had me go with him on his nighttime forays to other villages to seek from his old acquaintances help or hiding places.

Escape

One night we went to the Czuczman farm. We had to wade across the river Bug, then almost freezing. Today, I can see myself wading in the black water with my rags pulled up to my neck, in the piercing cold and dark, struggling to keep up with Jacob and finally reaching the far shore. All this happened in utter silence, to prevent discovery. It is hard for me to understand how my body took this punishing cold without a trace of ailment. We stumbled onward at night, covered in the dripping wet skimpy rags we wore for clothes, in shoes soaked with water. I followed Jacob like a little animal, knowing only fear, cold and hunger.

Jacob somehow found his way, mostly by instinct. There were no laid-out streets, and if there were any, we had to avoid them. There were no street lights in Busk, or in any of its surrounding villages. Electricity had come to Busk only just before the War.

Amid the barking of angry dogs, we arrived at the farm. Mr. Czuczman came out carrying a small kerosene lamp. He recognized Jacob, opened the door and let us in the house. He invited us to come close to the roaring fireplace and he and Jacob talked. We warmed our bones and dried our shoes and rags before the fireplace. We were given a bowl of pirogen floating in butter with sour cream. It was heaven on earth.

I stayed a couple of days with Jacob at the Czuczman barn. But Mr. Czuczman was afraid to let us hide there for long. And Tauba, my mother and Tulu needed to be hidden, too. And that meant Jacob and I had to go back to the others and keep searching for help to save us.

On another night, Jacob and his wife Tauba went to see what they could arrange with Mr. Turkiewicz in the village of Kupcze. Mr. Turkiewicz fed them and let them stay for a few days, but then he was afraid to keep them. So Jacob and Tauba had to leave.

As they walked along a dark country lane on their way back to us, three Ukrainian militiamen on bicycles suddenly appeared. They were returning to Busk from a village. One of them, taking a closer look at Jacob and Tauba, yelled out, "Zydy! Zydy!" They jumped off their bicycles. Jacob bolted and got away safely. One militiaman caught Tauba. He rode with her sitting on the crossbar at first, and then for the rest of the way marched her alongside. Once in Busk, they threw Tauba in jail. She was interrogated and beaten in their attempt to force her to reveal the hiding places of other Jews.

Jacob, in desperation, tried to get Tauba out. He contacted Mr. Czuczman for help and, in turn, Mr. Komendiuk. While behind bars in our small, primitive Busk jail, Tauba recalled hearing for several days a low voice calling her name, urging her to come over to the window. The caller claimed to be there to offer help, but Tauba, fearing a trap, did not appear at the window.

While Tauba was in jail, Jacob tried all his connections to get her out. It was Mr. Komendiuk who had come to the jail calling out to Tauba to come to the window, so that he could tell her how to escape. But nothing came of it.

Eventually, however, Tauba did escape through the roof. This was how it happened. The jail was a small, drab structure with small windows covered with heavy black iron bars. On the side was a small yard adjacent to the local courthouse. My maternal grandmother's house was across from this compound. Farther down the street was the lumberyard belonging to my mother and her brothers, including Jacob and Tulu. Still farther down was Herman's newly constructed house. And farther still, the road led to the railway station of Krasne-Busk.

Often as a child I was nearby the jailhouse when I went to visit or play in the lumberyard. One time, on my mother's insistence, I ran there to show my uncles the good grades I had received at the end of the school year. Sometimes, before the war, I would glue myself to the jailhouse fence in the hope of glimpsing the prisoners as they were led out for their walks in the prison yard. Another time, not far from the jailhouse, a young Ukrainian man, riding his horse while carrying his brand-new police uniform, fell to the ground as a truck drove by and caused the panic-stricken horse to bolt. I knew that man could be my tormentor, yet I could still feel sorry for him.

Another time, before the Ghetto was formed, while I was walking in front of the jail with my beloved little Shayele, nicknamed Siuniu, Rachel's four-year-old boy, he spontaneously tightened his lips knowing that he was passing a sinister place. He then looked up at me with his big, black, inquisitive, clever eyes seeking my approval and the kisses that I then gave him.

This was the jail where, before leaving Busk, the Russians had shot and killed several imprisoned Ukrainian Nationalists. This was the jailhouse into which my dear father and my brother Lonek were thrown after they were caught. For those Jews flushed out from their hiding places or caught escaping from the Ghetto, this was the last stop before the Jewish cemetery and execution.

By the time Tauba was locked up there, my father and Lonek were already dead. In a cell separate from the Jews were some ordinary prisoners, petty thieves or drunks. While these prisoners were let out in the yard, someone threw a package into their cell. One of the Jewish victims ran in, grabbed the package and found inside, embedded in loaves of bread, a file and a small pair of metal shears. He exclaimed to the others, men and women together, "Oy! We are saved!"

They went to work. They carved an opening in the ceiling. Then one or two inmates climbed up to the attic. There, they cut an opening in the sheet-metal roof. Those who decided not to escape lent their shoulders as ladders for those who climbed up.

Tauba climbed up to the attic that night. Through the hole in the roof she jumped out of the prison. There was no fence on the side where

Escape

she jumped. Another woman, with whom Tauba had arranged to meet up later, broke her ankle as she fell to the ground and could not go on. Tauba left her injured companion groaning by the wall of the jail. Tauba never learned what happened to the others who escaped. We did not hear from any of them again, ever.

Tauba was in her early twenties, a sheltered young woman from our small shtetl. Busk and its immediate surroundings had a population of approximately 10,000, of whom 3,000 were Jews. In all her life she had not ventured out of the township of Busk. Now for the first time, she was completely alone, in the dark night, on unfamiliar, unlit country roads, a fugitive from jail, and condemned to death as a Jew. In her confusion and bewilderment she lost her bearings and wound up just before daybreak walking in the opposite direction from the one she had intended. She found herself in Krasne, by the railroad station. Krasne, although a village, had the railroad station because it lay on a straight line heading east from Lwów. Now there were German soldiers posted in the village and, of course, guards all around the station. Tauba realized her mistake.

She quickly turned around and ran in the opposite direction. Hiding in fields during the day, she continued her lonely trek toward the out-skirts of Busk. Miraculously, she ran across the Jewish cemetery. From there, she knew how to get to Mrs. Dawidowska's. The compassionate Mrs. Dawidowska took pity on her, let her in, embraced her, fed her and treated her like a baby, as Tauba recalled. She put her up in a safe place. Later on, Mrs. Dawidowska brought Tauba to a relative of hers, Mr. Malkiewicz, who lived in a village close to Busk. Through Mrs. Dawidowska's efforts, we also ended up for a time at Mr. Malkiewicz's farm, and there we were reunited with Tauba.

In the meantime Tulu or Jacob, alone or together, and at times with me going with either or both of them, spent nights seeking contacts and finding hiding places, as our situation grew worse and worse. Winter approached. Danger filled these forays into the wet, cold, black nights. Mere existence was dangerous enough, but at least while in hiding we were not exposed to the local human vultures, or to the elements, or to the roaming, hungry and barking dogs; nor was there the risk of drowning or getting lost. We ventured out only in the pitch-black night. The hounds in the villages barked ceaselessly, and we could never be sure on whose door we knocked. We had no specific addresses. There were no street names in the villages, or house numbers. Each house could have been a trap, each opened door an invitation to our end.

During one such nighttime foray, we could not help but walk past some houses and back yards of what had been my beloved Busk. How scared I was to cross those empty, ghost-like, yet so familiar yards and streets.

Life Death Memories

Now I was in front of the house of my dearest friend Shiulu. In former times, he had shown me how to connect to a tiny bulb two wires attached to a battery, so that the bulb would light up. He was so advanced, so curious. It was he who made the strongest wire hooks we used to attach to the Russian army trucks as we skated up the hill together. We both had our own sleds and our own skates. We considered ourselves more daring than the other fellows. We roamed the streets together and were partners in teasing the girls. Shiulu carved in wood and had all kinds of tools and gadgets. I admired his dexterity. I knew that he was more able than I. Among our friends, either he or I would become the leader in whatever we were all doing. We had sworn to each other to be friends forever. Now, in passing his house and his back yard where we used to play, I knew that Shiulu was gone, and his family was gone.

Then, dodging the looming memories, and rushing to get away from the haunted streets and yards of Busk, I urgently prayed God that He make all the new occupiers of the houses here do the man-woman thing. This would surely divert their attention from Jacob and my presence in their back yards.

One night we were all lying asleep atop piles of straw in the attic of Mr. Malkiewicz's barn. Mr. Malkiewicz climbed the attic ladder and woke me with his step. I made believe I was sleeping. I heard a shuffling in the straw, a resistance, a whispering, a pushing away. I did not know what to think, but I was seething with anxiety and anger. My father came to my mind. I thought, "My father's blood has not yet dried!" Did this man want something from my mother? As I think of it now, possibly nothing happened. Yet, this moment gnawed at me. It was like a festering sore for many years.

Our stay at the Malkiewiczes' came to an end. Tulu went out on a mission to try to find another place for us.

In the 1930s, Mr. Fedorski had been mayor of Busk. He had died before the War and left a widow, three daughters and a son Rysio, my age. The Fedorskis were Polish landowners, raising horses, cows, pigs, chickens and geese on their property. They had a large house, a good-sized back yard, tool sheds and two large barns. Compared to other farmers, the Fedorskis were rather well off. Mrs. Fedorska knew my family very well. She and my mother had attended elementary school together. I was Rysio's classmate in the Polish school before the War. He was blond, aristocratic-looking, and he was the teacher's pet.

From the Malkiewicz farm, Tulu headed outside Busk toward his last hope, the Fedorski place. He arrived during the night. Mrs. Fedorska came out at his knock. Tulu told her that we were at the end of the tether, that she was our last hope. In fact, as my mother later said, he even declared, in desperation, that he would not budge from her doorstep unless she helped us. He begged her to exhaustion. He appealed to her human decency, that as a God-fearing person she was bound, yes, obligated to help, to let us hide on her property. Mrs. Fedorska relented. Then Tulu came for us with the good news that we would be given shelter in one of Mrs. Fedorska's barns.

Stealthily, during the black night, we made our way to the Fedorski farm. Our group was still my mother, Tulu, Jacob, Tauba and I. We settled down behind bales of hay in the attic of one of the barns. There was food and drink. Days passed.

I spent the days looking out through cracks between the boards, observing the yard below. I came to recognize the individual roosters and chickens. I marveled at and envied the carefree cows and the screeching, mud-wallowing pigs. I became familiar with the routine and activities of the farm: the constant cleaning of the barns, the regular milking of the cows, the walking of the horses in the yard, the chopping of potatoes for the pigs, the filling of the trough, the repairs. And of course I waited anxiously for some food and drink to come up to us in the attic.

At times I saw the beautiful Fedorski girls coming and going. Hidden and secretly, I gazed down through the cracks in the attic floor and often saw poor Rysio come into the barn. I watched him with curious excitement. He, poor Rysio, was sure that he was alone. He kept crossing himself, like a devout Catholic, and prayed compulsively, with his hands tightly clasped together. He kneeled facing the barn wall and recited prayers as though facing an altar.

He would run into the barn frequently and unexpectedly, appearing to be driven, and pray feverishly. Then, as quickly, he would run out, as if in fear of discovery. At prayer, he was in a trance. I could not help a sense of guilt, thinking that perhaps we, the hidden Jews, were the cause of his anxiety.

Escape

Mrs. Fedorska had a brother, Albert, a deaf-mute with other handicaps. He was our liaison, carrying food up to our attic hideout. Though he could not talk or hear, from his eyes, facial expression and demeanor it was clear that he fully understood the dangerous situation we were all in.

As we became more settled in and familiar with the place, Mrs. Fedorska became more open with us. To our greatest surprise she revealed that in her second barn there were two or three young Jewish men in hiding as well. These were among the last of the escapees from the Ghetto. They were part of the group of Jews left by the Germans to collect all that remained from the homes of the exterminated. As they told us, their job was to go from house to house in search of valuables, furs, clothing, even dishes. They were told to collect anything of value. It was all delivered to the German compound to be sorted: jewelry and silver were placed in boxes, salvageable items such as clothing and furs were bundled up,

dishes went into crates. This inventory was read-
ied for shipment to Germany. Anything of paper,
books, photographs, albums, prayer books, were
dumped on the floor of the main Jewish temple.

In searching through the empty homes, the
ghost-filled homes, the cleaning crew found
surprises. They found Mr. Weissblitt's body
hanging, strung up by his belt. They found other
dead bodies.

Then there was the little Rosen boy. He and
his family lived next door to my paternal grandparents' house, which was in the center of town,
in the rynek. Little Rosen was a small boy, approximately five or six years old. His nickname was a
bren faier, in Yiddish, the spark. He was always
swift, like a squirrel, and mischievous. His face
was freckled and his hair red.

As the cleanup crew came into the Rosen
house and up to the attic, there, on a beam, lay little Spark, stretched out. When a Jewish worker
nudged him to come off the beam, little Spark

Escape

Rosen wouldn't budge. The German and Ukrainian murderers came up to see what was going on. It took the efforts of several Germans and Ukrainians finally to pry little Spark off the beam. Spark clung to that beam as if he had been nailed to it and would not let go. A superior, brute force had to pry him loose and get him out. As he was dragged from the attic, he cried and kicked and scratched his captors. Finally, on this sunny day in May 1943, they shot Spark Rosen to death in front of his house.

The young men in the other barn gave us additional details of my beloved father's and Lonek's last days. On leaving the attic schron they were caught, by either the Germans or the Ukrainian militias, as they tried to run from the Ghetto. They were put in the Busk jail. We were told they had an opportunity to get away. I do not recall whether the opportunity was to run from the jail, or whether my father and Lonek expected to be assigned to cleanup work in the Ghetto and possibly to escape then. But my father had hope left in him. He could not believe that either he or his emaciated son Lonek would be killed. Perhaps he believed in miracles, or was he just too shocked and resigned, as neither was guilty of anything. What was happening?

He may have weighed the options. By not escaping he would show his captors his trustworthiness and reliability; and he and Lonek would be kept alive, put to work and not be killed. Anyway, what were the chances of finding help in the outside world? Such was the thinking among the victims in the jail and on the work crews. Some did take their chances and escaped. This was what Tauba did. She is the only one of the Jews of whom we know who, caught after the Judenrein of the Ghetto and put in the Busk jail, escaped and survived.

Towards the end of May 1943, the horse-drawn wagon pulled up to the jail. My beloved father, only forty-two years old, and my beloved brother Lonek, fifteen years old, were shoved into the wagon. My dearest, innocent father and my soul-mate, my brother, crouched in the wagon, under guard, as the horses pulled away. They knew the road well, and the destination became clear. How could it be otherwise?

From the jailhouse the road was rather straight. It crossed the bridge over our river Bug, then ran past the castle of the Hrabia Badeni. Then downhill, where I used to hook onto the Russian military trucks as they heaved up the steep grade, and past the burned-out Russian tank. Making a right turn onto Ulica Tarnowskiego, the horses pulled the carriage with its hapless victims to our Jewish cemetery. Soon they approached the house where my father, my Chuny, my Lonek and I were born. Then they passed by our house, still standing, the house where we were all raised. Not far away was the place where, for them, eternity began.

Life Death Memories

My father and brothers and even my grandfather had been born in Busk. Before my father and Lonek were put on the wagon, were they given a last meal? Were they subjected to more indignities? Were they offered some calming words? Were you crying, my father and Lonek? Did you, my father, console him? Did they let you embrace and cling to each other? Perhaps your tears commingled as you pressed your faces to each other. Perhaps this calmed you some. Perhaps you continued to have faith in God and prayed, and perhaps this had a steadying effect. My dearest father, my dearest Lonek, I will never know these answers, nor why all this had to happen. I do know that when you arrived at the Jewish cemetery, you were ordered to dig your grave. You were sprayed with bullets. You fell together into the pit you had to dig.

Via Dolorosa, Ulica Tarnowskiego, the Street of Pain. The Christians reenact yearly the Stations of the Cross along the Via Dolorosa in

Escape

Jerusalem. To me this symbolizes man's cruelty to man. I still feel that the tragic image of a crucified, bleeding Christ on the Cross should evoke compassion. To see the One in human form nailed there. To feel the terror of the image and of the event. The suffering, the pain! Should not that have taught the believers a lesson?! A lesson not to be cruel, not to inflict pain, not to kill. And yet just the opposite lesson grew so often from this symbol. Yes, I was aware even as a child of certain religious convictions which were held by non-Jews. It was a mystery to me and always frightening. I knew that Jews were said to have killed Christ. How scary all this was to me.

On the belt buckles of the German SS and the German soldiers was the motto Gott mit Uns. God with the murderers! Where were the priests, the intelligentsia, the Pope, yes, where was God?

My father Tobias Hecht, my Chuny, my Lonek, Hanusia, Shayele, Shiulu, Isaac, Rachel, Moiszaly, Heniek, Spark Rosen, my grandparents, cousins, friends, my little friends from the chaider with their payes and their observant families: they were the first to go. My friends from the Hebrew school. Mina, her sister Bertha and husband and child. Tescia, Laiser, and the millions who were never, anywhere, mentioned, except as one in a huge number. They were not revolutionaries; they did not come to save or change the world. They did not even have any claims to territories or to present-day civil rights. They merely wanted to live their lives.

But the German and Ukrainian executioners would not have it. In each area occupied by the German armies, including Estonia, Latvia, Lithuania, Poland, Russia, Yugoslavia and France, the Germans had local helpers in their enterprise of eliminating Jews merely because they were born Jews. And thus do I recite these events, in order to leave some trace of at least a few among the millions murdered.

Escape

This is to ease my conscience. And I must proclaim to those so cruelly murdered that they were so much more worthy than I. There are monuments for those turned to ashes at Auschwitz, Belzec, Majdanek, Bergen-Belsen, Birkenau, Treblinka, and hundreds of other death factories and unmarked mass graves. Here let a few individual names radiate from my store of memories, as well as the memories of all of my fellow Jews from the small shtetlach of what was our Galicia, in Southern Europe. In that way, and in your reading of Them, my dear reader, some element of Them will remain. Yes, a whole world I was born into once existed, and this whole world was suddenly turned to nothing, except for what remains in our memories.

Being in the habit of looking out through the cracks in the attic of the barn wall and onto the Fedorskis' yard, I was shocked to notice a contingent of German SS and Ukrainian Nationalist militia hastily entering the house. The uniformed men spread out and surrounded the barns and yard. I became paralyzed with fear. With a frantic hand gesture, I alerted the others in the attic. They understood and flattened their bodies on the floor. The noise level from the outside increased.

The German and Ukrainian expletives were loud and clear, and all too familiar. I was sure this was the end! Instinctively I stretched out my body as flat as possible on the floor. Now and then, to see what was happening, I lifted my head slightly. I saw the young Jewish men being led out of the other barn. Then I saw a Ukrainian militiaman run into our barn. He grabbed the ladder leaning against the stack of hay and started to climb up. I stopped breathing. I lifted my head a little higher and, through my nearly closed eyes, saw the top of the ascending militiaman's cap. Just then a thundering shout came from the direction of the main house: "We found the Jews!" Upon hearing this the militiaman halted his climb, as if stopped by a magic force. He stood there on the ledge for another split second. Then he started down the ladder and ran into the main house. We were saved.

In a hiding place in the main house, the murderers had just discovered another group of Jews. Mrs. Fedorska had been hiding two other Jewish families, five persons in all. We knew nothing about this. These were the Heller and Graff families. Of the five people, there was one little girl, two or three years old. She was not even in the hiding place during this. She had been running around at play in one of Mrs. Fedorska's rooms. All of them, including the baby and Mrs. Fedorska as well, were led away. The Jews were taken directly to the Jewish cemetery. They were all shot to death and thrown into a common grave. Mrs. Fedorska was taken to the police station.

Her teenage daughters and Rysio wailed for their mother. Their uncle Albert, Mrs. Fedorska's brother, ran about in a panic, gesturing and groaning like a wounded animal.

175

Mrs. Fedorska remained in the police station until the following day. On prior occasions she had made friends with some of the SS officers. She spoke some German and was known and well regarded by the Germans and even the Ukrainians. And while the SS were waiting for instructions about what to do with her, a drunken guard left the police station door open. Mrs. Fedorska, having great faith in Holy Mary, Mother of her God, and having prayed all day and night and believing in miracles, took the open door to be a sign to leave promptly. So she walked out and headed directly home.

Once there, she immediately gathered up her children and whatever she could take with her. They fled to the village of Angelowka, to her distant relatives the Kubalskis and Sokols. Her brother remained on the farm. A few days later, the SS came to look for her.

Next door to the Fedorski farm there lived the Zalipskis, a mother and her two grown bachelor sons. Tulu knew the family well. They were Ukrainians. For some reason there was continual rancor between the Fedorski family and the Zalipskis. Mrs. Fedorska at one time expressed the suspicion that the Zalipskis had betrayed her to the SS. In any event, on the night following the raid on the Fedorski farm, Jacob, Tulu, Tauba, my mother and I clandestinely entered the Zalipski barn. Several days later, Tulu revealed our presence to Thomasz Zalipski. He did not need to be told of our plight. Though very anxious, he permitted us to stay in the barn for another several days.

Mr. Zalipski told us about Mrs. Fedorska's escape and release. Jacob found her brother Albert and gave him a written message for her, begging her for help. This saintly woman, Mrs. Fedorska, did indeed help again. She prevailed upon Mr. Kubalski to come for us at night. He took us to a hiding place in the barn he had with his son-in-law Mr. Sokol, in the village of Angelowka.

Life Death Memories

During this period, the winter of 1943-44, Poles themselves were fleeing these areas of the Ukraine. They were afraid both of the local Ukrainians and of the Russians, who seemed to be winning the War. Large convoys of Poles headed west, to the Polish side of the country. The Fedorski family later joined one such convoy to resettle on the western side of the river San, which was Poland proper.

The Kubalski family consisted of husband and wife and their three daughters, two of them teenagers. The oldest of the daughters was married to Mr. Wladyslav, or Wladek, Sokol. Mrs. Kubalska was a petite, beautiful woman. Rumors were that the young, handsome son-in-law Wladek was in love with his mother-in-law. He himself, and, indirectly, the Kubalski family, were classified as Volksdeutsche, that is, people of ethnic German background. There were several such families in the village of Angelowka. That was why Mr. Sokol wore a special type of

178

black uniform. He was authorized to carry a rifle, and indeed he walked around with his rifle slung on his shoulder.

To our great surprise we learned that in a separate hiding place the Kubalskis and Sokols were hiding Mrs. Stoltzenberg with her two sons. Of course we knew them from Busk. The boys were sixteen and eighteen years old.

We came to the Kubalski-Sokol hideout around Christmas, 1943. It was the Christians' season of joy. One day Mr. Sokol called me into the house, which during the daytime was a risky thing to do. Crossing the yard on my way to the house I felt a pain in my knees. I could hardly stretch my legs, having been in a crouching position under the hay for days. Wladek prepared a hot bucket of water and made me wash myself. He cut my hair. He and his wife Maria and the Kubalskis and their other daughters were all there. The girls looked at me with amazement. It felt strange to be the object of their curiosity.

The hosts bade me sit down at the table and gave me a hearty meal. Here I was, sitting at a table. I had not had this experience since before the dreadful day of May 21, 1943. As the young Kubalski girls stared at me, I couldn't look back. Was I a hunted animal? How does one sit at a table? How does a starving person eat without gulping down the food? How does one hold a spoon, a knife, a fork? How does one eat at a table while people stare? How does one acknowledge one's place as a guest and show appreciation? How does one speak a mistrusted language, yet try to speak it without an accent? I felt strange, bewildered to be among people, in a house, in the open, in the daytime and so uncomfortable.

Suddenly there was a commotion. A contingent of German soldiers from the front had pulled into the village, and several rode up to the Kubalski farm with their horses and wagons. Before I had a chance to finish my meal I was shoved under the bed. A couple of German soldiers came into the house with their dog. They were boisterous and demanded food and schnapps. Food and drink for them came to the table, while the dog sniffed around. The dog in fact nudged me while I was lying stiff and motionless under the bed. Finally, the soldiers left with their dog, and I was called out. I could breathe again.

My hosts, my saviors, were shaken by the experience. I went back to my tomb in the barn under the hay.

One side of the barn was stacked up with hay and straw. Underneath this mass of forage they had carved out a space for us. During the day we had to stay crouched up. At night we crawled out, one at a time, to straighten out our bodies and legs. We dared walk only inside the barn, and only during the night.

By this time, the Germans were retreating from the eastern front. There was military movement all around us. Mr. Sokol or Mr. Kubalski would come into the barn and mutter, as if talking to himself, about activities at the front. As the German retreat from the eastern front became ever more obvious, our situation became more precarious. Bands of Ukrainians were burning the homes and barns of Polish farmers and forcing them to flee. It was what has come to be called ethnic cleansing.

We did no more than merely exist, in a state of constant fear, hunger and great discomfort, in a continuous, numbing pain. The winter of 1944 was agonizingly slow in passing. Our hopes for survival fluctuated, depending on rumors from the front, the struggle between the antagonistic Ukrainian and Polish populations, the availability of food, the good will of our hosts, and, of course, their reaction to their very real fears. More and more Poles were leaving, and the Kubalski and Sokol families, too, were preparing to abandon their home and go west. Still, we survived the winter of 1943-44.

Escape

The snow started to melt. It was March 1944.

We could hardly breathe in our entombment behind and under the hay. By placing our ears to the ground we could hear the explosions of bombs and artillery. This was music to us. As days progressed, more soldiers passed through the village. Then, soldiers, horses and equipment started to settle in, field kitchens were set up. Some troops even bivouacked inside the village itself. This portended an end to our present existence.

Now, a new danger! German soldiers with horses came to stay at the farm. Mr. Kubalski ran into the barn. He was panting, and, as if talking to himself, said that the barn and the hay had been requisitioned and that military horses would be stationed in the barn. Fearing that we would be discovered, the Kubalskis and Sokols were going to leave their house. Soon after, soldiers came into the yard to set up a field kitchen, and then several of them with their horses entered the barn. The horses started nibbling on the hay. A few soldiers actually climbed on top of the pile of fodder. Beneath the stacks of hay we were huddled, petrified.

The soldiers laughed and cavorted and made jokes about stupid Polish farmers and used all kinds of profanities. They were sitting on the hay above us, and their horses were nibbling at the hay on either side of us. As our protective walls were dwindling and about to collapse on us, Mr. Kubalski suddenly appeared and remonstrated with the German officer. He told him not to allow the horses to eat all the hay: after all, none would be left for his cows and his own horses, and they would all starve. Mr. Kubalski argued vehemently. They eventually relented and pulled their horses away.

Later on that day, Mr. Kubalski, as if speaking to his wife, but really for us to hear, said that by that very night we must run away into the woods.

We survived the day. Night fell. The German soldiers were sleeping in the main house and guards were stationed in the yard. The horses were

Escape

in the barn. Our physical condition was such that we could hardly walk, let alone run. But we knew that the time had come to escape from the barn if we could, no matter what. In our weakened state, we crawled painfully out from under the haystacks and let ourselves down to the floor. It was completely dark. We felt our way towards the barn doors. The horses were slowly waking from slumber. In a panic we discovered that the barn doors were padlocked from the outside. The German military guard was only paces away in the yard.

We stopped cold at the locked barn doors. The horses were at our backs. We were now completely exposed, not even protected by the flimsy shelter of hay. We were stunned, disoriented and about to give up when, like a lightning bolt, a horse kicked the barn doors wide open. Galvanized by the horse's violent blow, we tore through the yard and into the adjoining woods. And just then, the village dogs started to bark,

185

searchlights lit up all around us, the Germans began yelling and bullets flew.

Following us, the Stoltzenbergs ran from their hiding place. A bullet struck the eighteen-year-old boy. But the younger brother escaped and reached the woods with us.

Tauba ran into the woods but became separated from us. We did not know what happened to her. She eventually found her way to Mr. Komendiuk and to the Smahas, who led her to a group of Jews hiding in the neighboring woods. We were not reunited with her until our liberation.

Mrs. Stoltzenberg stayed by her wounded son. The Germans arrested both and kept them overnight. The following morning they told Mrs. Stoltzenberg to leave by herself. She refused to go without her son. He and his mother were shot to death on the spot.

The Kubalski and Sokol families had left their farm the day before our escape, but they lingered in the neighborhood. Several days later, Mr.

Escape

Kubalski and Wladek Sokol found us in the woods. They helped us for another few weeks, but then they abandoned their home and farm and departed with a convoy to the west. Before that, however, they brought Michal to us, a cultivated Ukrainian man who, at great risk to himself, continued to help us.

Michal brought Hanka to our group. Hanka was a young Jewish girl whom he was hiding. They were lovers. Michal often came to visit Hanka in private. He also came to see us and brought us food and news from the front.

Another person who joined our group was a young Jewish man born and raised in one of the nearby villages. His name was Laiser. He knew people in the villages and was familiar with the layout of the forest. He could get food and was willing to share whatever he found. To me, to all of us, under the circumstances, he was a pillar of strength and object of admiration.

187

One evening my mother showed me where Laiser had hidden some bread. She may have told me to go and take a piece. But there were others among us as well. There was the Stoltzenberg boy, there was Tulu, there was Hanka. There were rodents and squirrels. But reluctantly I did take a piece of the bread.

The following day Laiser discovered that some of his bread was missing. He told Jacob, who immediately decided that I was the thief. In a wild rage, he pounced on me and struck me in the face. My pain and shame overwhelmed me. Should I survive, I vowed I would take my revenge on Jacob. I was also angry with my mother. She should have let me die of starvation rather than have shown me where Laiser kept his bread.

And yet, were it not for my mother's devotion, I would not have survived. When she told me about Laiser's bread, was she afraid that I was on the verge of starving? Had the cold, the wet and the lack of food lasted just a little longer, I and perhaps all of us would have died of one or the other. I was close to looking like a skeleton. The small fire that was our source of warmth was, for safety, kindled only at night. By the time the food was shared among all of us it was mere crumbs. Only the pounding of the cannon as the front drew nearer kept me from utter resignation.

Regrettably, Jacob's hitting me marred my relationship with him through the years. I did not have the courage or wisdom to talk over our shared past with him. To him I remained an ungrateful boy, while I remained in my own mind the trembling, injured victim in the woods. In my relationship with him, as in my relationship with my mother, I failed to grow up. Even today, I act as the child with Tauba. I was not man enough to give Jacob the credit due him for his vital deeds in enabling me to survive. And while I created a new personality, and even a new name for myself, and worked incessantly to create a new life and future, Jacob remained mired in the past. Additionally, as our paths and fortunes diverged, he harbored a certain suspicion and possibly resentment of me. I beg his forgiveness now. He was a good man who could not let go of the past. He hid his disappointments and pain in alcohol. He died a broken man.

But my mother, my mother was totally single-minded in watching out for her own. The relationship between my mother and me was never quite normal, although our loyalty to each other remained indestructible. The love and affection between us remained buried under layers of shame, guilt and confusion. For my part, I felt guilty that I had survived my father and my two brothers. My mother on the other hand was sure that I had forgotten the past, and she resented this. She could not understand my focus on building a new future for myself. Whenever I wished to share with her my accomplishments she wished me to share with her the pain of her loss.

To our group in the woods it was clear that the Russian-German front was rapidly moving closer.

Escape

The weather became warmer. I would place my ear to the ground and hear the explosions of bombs and artillery get louder each day.

It was a beautiful warm day when Laiser came back from the village and told us that Michal had been killed by his own people. His Ukrainian friends had discovered that he had possibly had a part in helping Jews in the forest. So they killed him.

We heard frogs croaking. Tulu, having lived and studied in Vienna, knew that frogs were edible and in fact were considered a delicacy. So he made me go with him to a pond in the woods to catch some frogs. No sooner did we reach the clearing and the bog where we had heard the frogs, than shots were fired at us. We turned and ran into the woods. We were already behind bushes and trees when Tulu fell to the ground crying for help. Instantly I pulled off my torn, dirty shirt and tied his bleeding wound. He recovered fully, though before the War Tulu had suffered

191

from tuberculosis. But during our ordeals, it stayed dormant.

We heard rumbling sounds from the highway, and more gunfire. We felt that liberation was imminent. Laiser went to the village to see what was happening. On his way back to our hiding place, a bullet struck him. A retreating German patrol had ended another beautiful life.

We lifted our broken, emaciated bodies and crawled slowly, cautiously toward the sound of the tanks and trucks. We stumbled to a ditch by the side of the highway and collapsed into it. On the road appeared trucks emblazoned with red banners carrying Russian soldiers. We struggled up from the ditch and stood on the highway. A Red Army truck stopped. The soldiers picked us up, and we rode along with them for a while; and then they left us off in at what had been, not so very long ago, my beloved Busk. On being liberated, my feelings were not of joy, but of utter exhaustion and numbness. From the rynek I walked over

Escape

to Ulica Tarnowskiego and towards my house. But there was no house, only ruins of a house.

All that stood upright on the property were the two trees, the apple tree and the walnut tree, that I had so much cherished. I was struck with the notion that as if in defiance the trees had flourished during my absence. Their trunks had fattened up; the leaves were full and dark green. Wildflowers and weeds were growing all around the trees and out of the ruins.

I was too tired to cry or to think. I turned back towards the rynek, where we had claimed an abandoned apartment for our emaciated bodies. After several days the Russian military authorities took Jacob away under guard, to an army post to be drafted into the Red Army. On the way there, instinctively realizing that his future in uniform was to be cannon fodder for the battles now raging, he bolted and ran from the poor young soldier who was to deliver him to the draft office. It became clear that there was no longer anything for us in Busk.

Epilogue

We went to Lwów, and again we squatted in an empty apartment. Word came from Jacob that he was now in Przemysl, the border town separating Poland from what was now the Soviet Ukraine. After several months in Lwów we secretly smuggled ourselves to Przemysl. We lived there several months and then moved on west, to Lublin for about the same length of time, and then to Krakow.

In Krakow an organized Jewish community was sprouting up. A Zionist youth group invited me to join. I grasped that the Polish people didn't welcome us Jews any more than had the Ukrainians or the Russians. And therefore I became convinced that only Palestine, now Israel, would be the place to settle. In spite of my mother's entreaties, I did join a Zionist youth group, left my mother, and left Krakow, in an undercover transport operation bound for a kibbutz in Germany.

I did not adjust well to the communal lifestyle at the kibbutz. At the same time I had pangs of guilt over having left my mother. She in the meantime left Poland and moved to Vienna. Her tearful letters and messages beseeched me to return to her. They were filled with her plans to find a way for us to emigrate to America. Eventually I relented. I left the kibbutz, left Germany, and came to live with her in Austria. In time, she and I became classified as DPs (Displaced Persons) under special immigration laws passed by the U. S. Congress. And it was in this category of immigrants that we finally came to the United States in July of 1948.

List of Names

Badeni, Hrabia The Count Badeni, local large landowner and brewer of Piwo Badeni

Chaya _____ Author's great-aunt (mother's aunt)

Ciupka Author's nickname

Czuczman, Mr. A farmer, friend of Jacob Goldberg

Dawidowska, Mrs. A farmer's widow, who helped during the escape

Endek The National Democrats, a Polish fascist political organization

Fedorski Prominent farm family, of help during the escape

Fedorski, Albert Handicapped brother of Mrs. Fedorska

Fedorski, Rysiu Author's classmate in Polish school

Fink, Pepcia Author's friend

Flieser Refugee family billeted with the Hechts

Life Death Memories

Goldberg, Abraham	Author's uncle (mother's brother)
Goldberg, Hanusia	Author's first cousin (uncle Herman and Aunt Mina's daughter)
(Goldberg), Henia ___	Author's aunt (mother's half-sister)
Goldberg, Herman	Author's uncle (mother's brother)
Goldberg, Itzchak	Author's uncle (mother's brother, called "The Philosopher")
(Goldberg), Iziu	Author's aunt Rachel's step-brother
Goldberg, Jacob	Author's uncle (mother's brother)
(Goldberg), Laiser	Author's step-uncle (mother's step-brother)
Goldberg, Mina	Author's aunt by marriage (uncle Herman's wife)
Goldberg, Oscar	Author's maternal grandfather (mother's father)
Goldberg, Rachel	Author's aunt by marriage (uncle Abraham's wife; cousin Shayele's mother)
Goldberg, Ruth	Author's first cousin (uncle Tulu and aunt Salka's daughter)
Goldberg, Salka	Author's aunt by marriage (uncle Tulu's wife and Mr. Weissblitt's daughter)
Goldberg, Shayele	Author's first cousin (uncle Abraham's son)

List of Names

Goldberg, Tauba	Author's aunt by marriage (uncle Jacob's wife)
Goldberg, Tulu	Author's uncle (mother's brother)
Goldberg, Yoynele	Author's first cousin (Jacob and Tauba's son)
Graff	Jewish family also hiding at the Fedorski farm
Hanka_____	Jewish girl in author's group just before liberation; Michal's girl-friend
Hecht, Chuny	Author's eldest brother
Hecht, Fanka	Author's aunt by marriage (uncle Yichiel's wife)
Hecht, Heschel	Author's paternal grandfather (father's father)
Hecht, Klara	Author's mother
Hecht, Lonek	Author's older brother
Hecht, Moiszaly	Author's uncle (father's brother)
Hecht, Peria	Author's paternal grandmother (father's mother)
Hecht, Rysio	Author's first cousin (uncle Yichiel's son)
Hecht, Tobias	Author's father
Hecht, Yichiel	Author's uncle (father's brother)
Heller	Jewish family also hiding at the Fedorski farm

Life Death Memories

Hesiu _____	Author's childhood friend
Israel	Author's Hebrew name
Januszek, ____	Cruel labor foreman at Krasne
Komendiuk, Mr.	Ukrainian, a school friend of Jacob Goldberg, of help during the escape
Kubalski	Farmers, related to Mrs. Fedorska
Laiser _____	Jewish man, joined author's group just before liberation
Laybele, _____	One of the Jewish Ghetto police
Malkiewicz	Farm family related to Mrs. Dawidowska
Michal _____	Ukrainian man, joined author's group just before liberation, Hanka's lover
Mordechai ___	Author's great-uncle (mother's uncle)
Rosen, "Spark"	A neighborhood boy in Busk
Schoychete	Ritual slaughterer of fowl
Shulu _____	Author's childhood friend
Smaha	Ukrainian farm family, Nationalists, of help during the escape
Sokol, Wladyslaw	Also called Wladek; son-in-law of the Kubalskis
Srulikel	Diminutive of Israel, author's

List of Names

	Hebrew name as used by grand-parents
Stoltzenberg	Jewish family also hiding at the Kubalski farm
Szeptytskiy, Andrei	Metrolopolitan of the Ukrainian Orthodox Church
Tarnowskiego, Ulica	Street in Busk where author lived at No. 9
Tescia _____	Author's friend
Turkiewicz, Mr.	Jacob Goldberg's co-worker, of help during the escape
Weissblitt, Mr.	Wealthy Busk industrialist, Salka Goldberg's father
Zabka	Author's and his brothers' pet dog
Zalipski, Thomasz	Adjacent farm neighbors of the Fedorskis

Notes

Stefan Bandera, leader of the Ukrainian Insurrectionary Army (UPA) fought in the underground against the Red Army, the Wehrmacht, and the Polish Home Army (AK).

Marshal Joseph Pilsudski was the Polish head of state and commander in chief of the Polish Army during the First World War (WWI). He presided over the liberation of Poland after WWI. He strove to secure independence by encouraging the emancipation of states lying between Poland and Russia, including Lithuania, Belorussia and the Ukraine.

The Ukrainian commander Ataman Semyon Petliura, head of the Ukrainian Directorate, collaborated with Pilsudski in this effort. He was assassinated in Paris in 1926.

The Sheptytsky Institute has published, together with the Canadian Institute of Ukrainian

Notes

Studies Press and the Basilian Press, Prof. Andrii Krawchuk's book on the social teaching of Metropolitan Andrei Sheptytsky. The book is entitled "Christian Social Ethics in Ukraine: The Legacy of Andrei Sheptytsky." A grant for this was offered by the Ukrainian Catholic Women's League of Canada (Toronto Eparchy Executive).

Metropolitan Andrei Sheptytsky (1865 – 1944) was during the War the head of the Uniate (Ukrainian Christian) church in Galicia.

His brother, Father Superior Kliment Sheptytsky (1869 – 1951), was also a Uniate priest and during the War was the archimandrite of the local Studite monasteries.

In 1942 Metropolitan Andrei wrote a letter, which has become famous, requiring his followers to cease persecuting the Jews. During the Aktion of late 1942, Andrei and Kliment managed to save several hundred Jewish children by hiding them in various places including Andrei's home and several monasteries.

Life Death Memories

Both brothers are being considered for saint-
hood.

The Endek were the National Democratic
political party of wartime Poland. They were
Nazi partisans.

The Organisation Todt (OT) was founded in
1938 under the leadership of Fritz Todt after
whom it was named. He led the OT until his
death in 1942. Albert Speer took over then and
ran it until 1945. Its mission during the early
1940s was construction of roads, concentration
camps and other facilities in territories occupied
by the Germans. Since most of its workers were
slave laborers and prisoners of war, the OT
worked closely with the Gestapo and the SS.

About the Author

Thomas T. Hecht was born in Busk, Poland (now Busk, Ukraine) on November 27, 1929. After the events recounted in this book, he and his mother had many adventures. After their liberation they sojourned in a number of towns, until finally they were admitted to New York in July 1948 under the Displaced Persons program. His first job as an apprentice auto mechanic led to other factory work. Though at first unable to speak English, he prepared through his night high school classes for City College and, later, Brooklyn Law School. He graduated with an LL.B in 1957, having worked full time throughout his education. He has practiced law in New York ever since.

Married and the father of two sons, both attorneys, he has three grandchildren. He is contemplating writing a continuation of his story.

About the Illustrator

Eric L. Binder was born in 1968 in Bogota, Colombia. Son of missionaries who translated portions of the Old and the New Testaments for the Wounaan people, he grew up in Panama speaking English, Wounmeu and Spanish. It was in the seventh grade that he knew he was going to be an artist. After graduating from the Ringling School of Art in Florida he moved to California and painted a 30 foot mural and created some life-size sculpture. He then freelanced for various companies illustrating licensed characters.

He is now pursuing figurative painting as his first love in art. He is inspired by Velasquez, Balthus and Ogata Korin to name just a few. He currently lives in Charlottesville, Virginia with his wife and three boys.

About the Publisher

In the late winter of 1999-2000, Adam B. Ulam, the Gurney Professor (Emeritus) of History and Political Science at Harvard University, founded and named Leopolis Press in partnership with his wife, Mary H. Burgwin Ulam. The name means Lion City and was the medieval Latin name of Lwów, Poland, Professor Ulam's birthplace and hometown. At the time Professor Ulam was terminally ill and in hospital. His goal was to ensure the satisfactory publication of his 20th and last book before his death. He died, however, on March 28, 2000, shortly before his book saw the light of publication.

Under Mary Ulam's direction, Leopolis Press in early 2001 published *Understanding the Cold War: A Historian's Personal Reflections*. For Transaction Publishers of Princeton New Jersey, Leopolis Press prepared a second edition with newly discovered biographical material. This will appear in early 2002.

The manuscript of *Life Death Memories* came to light through a chain of connections reaching back to Adam Ulam's childhood in Lwów.

Leopolis Press now looks forward to the publication in 2003 of an annotated edition of Ulam family letters written to renowned mathematician and Manhattan Project scientist Stanislaw Ulam (Adam Ulam's older brother) during 1936-1947. These letters will appear in Polish and German with translations into English.

Colophon

This first edition of *Life Death Memories* was prepared for printing by Mary Ulam, Robert Johnston, John Tytus, and Cyane Williams, using QuarkXpress. The font is 13 point Janson Text.

A first printing of 1,500 copies was done upon 60# Glatfelter Offset and printed and bound by Thomson-Shore, Inc., Dexter, MI.